EXECUTIVEness

The Power to Achieve Superior Leadership through Unconventional Approaches

A Guide to Today's Real-World Leadership Excellence

By

Pat Rojas

Dedication

For those who believe that leadership is beyond their reach, this book stands as a testament that leadership transcends limits and boundaries, a truth I've come to know intimately.

For those who believe they can elevate their leadership journey, may this book help you discover your path.

And for those who believe there's nothing more they can learn; may this book reveal the untapped potential within you.

So, to the dreamers and skeptics, believers and achievers, this book is dedicated to you. May its insights empower you to embrace your executive self with certainty, authenticity, and the unwavering belief that you can make a greater impact, no matter where you stand today!

Table of Contents

Preface

As I stand on the edge of embarking on this transformative journey with you, I'm reminded of the many years I've spent navigating the complex landscapes of the corporate world. Over three decades of experience have revealed a truth: the path to success isn't solely paved with knowledge, skills, or experience. Instead, it's a dynamic fusion of intuition, keen observation, and, intriguingly enough, a touch of "naiveté."

When I mention "naiveté," I am not talking about gullibility or a lack of knowledge but rather unawareness—being free from preconceived notions. As someone with rich multicultural experiences, having lived and worked in several countries, I defied categorization. I became a global citizen before the term was probably coined, embracing adaptability, cultural fluency, and a fearlessness that propelled me toward new horizons.

My professional journey was a thrilling one, spanning from administrative roles and business ownership to high-pressure sales and management positions. This trajectory led me to occupy influential roles at the highest levels. Today, I revel in the freedom of managing my own business and finding fulfillment in guiding others to unlock their professional potential.

Looking back, it wasn't just a combination of intuition, self-belief, and an unquenchable desire to learn that propelled me forward. It was also the ability to see opportunities in challenges, innovate, and lead with a sense of purpose. These elements combined to form what I call "*EXECUTIVEness*"—a fusion of intellect, emotional acumen, and the audacity to question conventions.

In the following pages, I share invaluable lessons learned from my diverse experiences. These are insights rarely mentioned in any book, distilled from my journey as a psychologist, corporate executive, and leadership mentor. I seek to convey that your path to leadership excellence is far from confined. It's about unveiling your *EXECUTIVEness*—a blend of boldness, creativity, and the ability to view leadership through a dynamic lens. By integrating these principles into your daily routine, you're nurturing the habit of questioning assumptions, approaching problems from multiple angles, and seeing humanity through a multifaceted perspective.

This book is not just a theoretical discussion; it's a hands-on guide to real-world strategies that can transform you into a visionary leader quickly and easily. By embracing these concepts, you're embarking on an exhilarating journey—one that promises to revolutionize your approach to leadership and cultivate a lasting impact.

I invite you to accompany me on this exploration of *EXECUTIVEness*—an indispensable guide crafted for those who dare to challenge the established norms, blaze their own trails, and lead with clarity, impact, and authenticity. As we journey together, let's harness the insights distilled from a career lived at the crossroads of knowledge, experience, and the art of unapologetically being ourselves. With these tools, you can accelerate your path to leadership success, making the impossible not only possible but attainable.

Introduction

In today's rapidly evolving global landscape, a new paradigm of leadership is emerging, one that transcends traditional notions of executive expertise. Welcome to "***EXECUTIVEness*** **- The Power to Achieve Superior Leadership through Unconventional Approaches**", your guide to real-world leadership excellence. Together, in the following pages, I invite you to redefine leadership in a dynamic, straightforward, and audacious manner.

Superior Leadership isn't just mastering a collection of skills; it's a philosophy that equips you to navigate the complexities of the corporate terrain with knowledge, adaptability, and an unyielding spirit. We're venturing into the realm of ***EXECUTIVEness***, a term I've coined to encapsulate the **fearlessness, awareness, boldness, effectiveness, openness, clearness, and willingness to accept change** that define today's outstanding leaders, unafraid of unconventional approaches.

However, this book isn't a theoretical talk; it's a practical guide to real-world strategies that have the power to transform you into a Superior Leader. By embracing this concept, you're embarking on an exhilarating journey, one that promises to revolutionize your approach to leadership and leave a lasting impact.

In the chapters ahead, you'll discover actionable steps designed to propel you beyond your comfort zone and immerse you in practical applications. These practices go beyond mere exercises; they are gateways to discovering your leadership prowess and pathways to drive meaningful change.

So, I invite you to join me on this journey as we explore the vast potential within you and awaken your own version of leadership excellence.

I am thrilled to share with you what I learned from experience, determination, and my unwavering pursuit of **EXECUTIVEness**.

Let's dive right in.

Chapter 1:

The Fusion of Skills and Emotions - Discovering the Core of *EXECUTIVEness*

In my early leadership journey, I experienced moments of accomplishment and clarity alongside times of uncertainty. Despite navigating diverse roles successfully, I reached a juncture, in my mid-thirties, where my career seemed to plateau. This realization triggered questions: Why now? What am I missing? Is this "it" for me? What am I doing wrong? What was the intangible element I had missed?

As someone who had surpassed many goals and achieved recognition, I suddenly felt uncomfortable and uneasy—I sensed a stagnation, a lack of intensity in my contributions. This led me to search for that elusive factor that would reignite my leadership trajectory and illuminate a new path toward excellence.

This revelation extended beyond mere technical prowess or emotional intelligence. It encompassed all the hidden elements that collectively define *EXECUTIVEness*—a concept I coined as I delved deeper into the dynamics of leadership.

EXECUTIVEness, as I've come to define it, is the fusion of intellect, emotional acumen, instinct, and boldness. It compels us to view leadership through a dynamic lens, by probing, inquiring, and discerning. It urges us to challenge the status quo, disrupt familiar patterns, and embrace the courage to explore uncharted territories.

In a world often fixated on quantifiable outcomes and immediate results, I realized the inadvertent neglect of the power of instincts, emotions, and human connections. These are not just gateways to understanding others but, more importantly, to understanding oneself—the acceptance and courage to act authentically.

My pursuit of fleeting and short-term victories and achievements had inadvertently distracted me from viewing challenges through diverse lenses and from transcending tactical minutiae to embracing a panoramic view of the bigger picture.

> LEADERSHIP IS NOT MERELY A JUXTAPOSITION OF TECHNICAL BRILLIANCE AND STRATEGIC THINKING. IT IS A DELICATE EQUILIBRIUM BETWEEN KEEN VISION, EXCEPTIONAL ADEPTNESS, AND PROFOUND EMOTIONAL RESONANCE—A NUANCED BALANCE THAT MANY, INCLUDING MYSELF, HAD UNDERESTIMATED.

1.1 The Delicate Interplay of Intellect, Gut and Emotion

In my early leadership journey, I made a common mistake: overemphasizing technical proficiency as the foundation of effective decision-making and strategic planning. My decisions were driven by my deep knowledge of my company, my team, our resources, goals, and challenges. I relied heavily on the "knowledge of things," inadvertently obscuring the human aspect of leadership.

This technical focus led to unintended consequences. By concentrating on precision and factual knowledge, I diminished my awareness of personal victories and struggles within my team, losing the ability to relate, inspire, and influence. The pursuit of results became a narrow path that overlooked emotional needs, ignored gut feelings, and prevented a comprehensive view of situations. My leadership was average, devoid of the depth that comes from understanding and connecting with people.

1.2 Striking a Balance: Rationality and Emotional Aptitude

Rationality allows us to weigh pros and cons, analyze data, foresee potential outcomes, and align choices with overarching goals. Rooting decisions in logic ensures they are well-considered, comprehensive, and forward-looking. However, leadership that overly prioritizes rationality might exude an aura of detachment. Leaders may be perceived as lacking empathy or disregarding the unique experiences and challenges faced by not only their teams, but also their superiors, peers, and customers. Such a perception can hinder trust, obstruct open communication, and weaken relationships at multiple levels within and outside the organization.

Conversely, an exclusive focus on emotions can lead to decisions devoid of rationality. I've witnessed instances where decisions swayed solely by emotions led to misinterpretations of facts and outcomes misaligned with organizational goals.

Effective leadership demands the capacity to harmonize these sometimes-opposing elements—making informed decisions while grasping and connecting with emotions, all without veering into impulsive or biased choices. The process of achieving results is driven by people. It requires recognizing their individual contributions, understanding their challenges, and fostering an environment where they feel valued and heard. This people-centric approach not only enhances team dynamics but also strengthens bonds with superiors, peers, and customers, facilitating a culture of mutual respect and open dialogue.

> IN ESSENCE, RESULTS ARE THE GOAL, BUT *EXECUTIVENESS* IS INHERENTLY PEOPLE-FOCUSED.

This delicate balance between rationality and emotional aptitude is what elevates leadership from average to extraordinary, driving sustainable success through deeply connected and motivated relationships at all levels of the organization.

1.3 Embracing Fearlessness and the Pursuit of Success

Another facet of *EXECUTIVEness* revolves around viewing leadership as a dynamic journey fueled by courage—a willingness to push boundaries and defy the grip of fear. This courage stems from a deep desire to succeed and create meaningful impacts, grounded in a firm belief in oneself.

This pursuit of excellence is not superficial; it's an unrelenting force that drives us toward the extraordinary. This ambition serves as a compass, guiding actions, decisions, and attitudes through challenges.

In my personal journey, I recognized that my innate fearlessness towards failure was a natural asset contributing to my career success. My experiences of living in different countries and immersing myself in diverse cultures taught me that in environments of constant change, errors, failures, and course corrections are intrinsic to growth.

Embracing uncertainty is pivotal for professional growth, where failure serves as a steppingstone rather than a dead end. Fearlessness isn't recklessness; it's calculated and grounded in situational awareness.

EXECUTIVENESS IS A BLEND OF UNYIELDING AMBITION, RISK-TAKING, AND EMOTIONAL PROWESS—A SPIRIT THAT INSPIRES EXCELLENCE AND INNOVATION, COMPELLING LEADERS TO CONFRONT CHALLENGES HEAD-ON AND EMPOWER THEIR TEAMS TO DO THE SAME.

1.4 The Fusion that Catalyzes Excellence

When intellect and emotion intertwine seamlessly, they create a constructive interaction that amplifies a leader's effectiveness. The ability to comprehend emotions, both in oneself and others, combined with analytical thinking, empowers leaders to navigate complex situations with empathy, trust, influence, and strategic insight.

This emotional awareness serves as a compass, guiding leaders through the intricate terrain of human interactions. It's about deciphering unspoken sentiments, understanding between the lines, and leveraging this insight to foster collaboration and cohesion.

Imagine grappling with a tough decision that could impact team morale. By integrating emotional awareness with analytical prowess, leaders don't just evaluate data and figures; they gauge the team's emotional pulse. This dynamic integration empowers leaders to make decisions that are data-informed and considerate of the human dimension, nurturing trust and loyalty.

Furthermore, this synergy doesn't merely enhance decision-making; it fosters a culture of authenticity. Being attuned to emotions allows leaders to communicate transparently, admit mistakes, and share victories in relatable ways. This openness encourages vulnerability among team members, fostering genuine connections and mutual respect.

The melding of intellectual and emotional aspects, in harmony with other pivotal traits, forges a dynamic interplay of unique skills, empowering leaders to make decisions that are not just logical but also empathetic, not just strategic but also innovative.

1.5 Propelling Personal and Collective Growth

The trajectory *of EXECUTIVEness* doesn't merely influence personal development but extends to the growth of teams and organizations. Emotional awareness enables leaders to cultivate trust, collaboration, and open communication—an environment that catalyzes the growth and development of all.

By delving into emotional intelligence, leaders become finely attuned to the needs and aspirations of their team members. This understanding empowers leaders to provide tailored guidance and support, nurturing the potential of each individual.

Imagine a leader who wields technical expertise while possessing a profound understanding of their team's emotions and motivations. Such leaders strategically delegate tasks, align team members with roles that resonate with their strengths, and foster a sense of purpose that inspires commitment and dedication.

This alignment transcends team boundaries, permeating the entire organization. When leaders inspire trust and transparency, these qualities shape organizational culture. Interactions become candid, hierarchies flatten, and collaboration flourishes—a harmonious ecosystem that nurtures innovation.

The integration of intellectual and emotional aspects, along with adaptability and audacity, empowers leaders with *EXECUTIVEness* to drive personal growth and that of their teams and organizations. By cultivating an atmosphere of trust and understanding, leaders initiate a ripple effect that amplifies the potential of every individual and shapes collective success.

As leaders ascend, they embody Superior Leadership that transcends guidance—it sparks a chain reaction of growth, innovation, and triumph.

1.6 The Nexus of Technical Mastery, Emotional Insight, Adaptability, and Audacity

EXECUTIVEness encapsulates the quintessence of leadership—a blend of technical prowess, emotional intelligence, adaptability, and audacity. It's about making informed decisions while understanding and connecting with emotions, without veering into impulsiveness or bias.

Imagine a leader proficient in technical skills but lacking emotional insight to connect deeply with their team. Such leaders excel in data-driven decisions but may struggle to inspire or motivate.

Conversely, a leader attuned to their team's emotions but lacking technical acumen may make decisions lacking depth and strategic insight. *EXECUTIVEness* bridges this gap, leveraging technical finesse as a foundation for empathy and understanding.

EXECUTIVEness demands embracing adaptability as fundamental to thriving in today's fast-paced corporate landscape. It's about audacity—the courage to chart unexplored territories, make unconventional decisions, and achieve remarkable outcomes.

The concept embraces the multifaceted nature of true leadership—the integration of intellectual and emotional aspects, in harmony with other pivotal traits, empowers leaders to make decisions that are not just logical but also empathetic, not just strategic but also innovative.

This fusion holds the key to elevating leadership to unparalleled heights—surmounting challenges, nurturing growth, and driving positive transformation.

1.7 Navigating *EXECUTIVEness*: Taking the Inaugural Step

Understanding the essence marks the beginning of transformational leadership. To embrace **EXECUTIVEness**, I invite you to embark on practical exercises:

Self-Reflection and Emotional Inventory: Dedicate moments to introspection. Reflect on recent decisions and interactions as a leader. Were choices primarily driven by logic or influenced by emotions? Identify instances where a balanced approach could enhance your leadership.

Scenario Analysis: Select a complex decision and scrutinize it from both technical and emotional perspectives. How did emotions impact your decision-making process? Use this exercise to explore the interplay between intellect and emotion in your leadership style.

> THE JOURNEY TO EXCELLENCE IS ONGOING. EACH STEP TOWARD EMBRACING *EXECUTIVENESS* PROPELS YOU CLOSER TO UNVEILING YOUR FULL POTENTIAL. BY INTEGRATING TECHNICAL MASTERY, EMOTIONAL INSIGHT, ADAPTABILITY, AND AUDACITY, YOU SET THE STAGE FOR UNPARALLELED PERSONAL AND COLLECTIVE GROWTH.

Chapter 2:

Tracing Your Unique Path: Impact of Past Experiences - Exploring Threads of Influence on Your Journey

Back in the early 2000s, after making headway in my leadership journey, I started feeling a nagging sense. While achieving milestones brought satisfaction, a deeper unease lingered – a feeling that I wasn't fully reaching my potential. Titles and recognition were there, yet the challenges felt predictable. The paths to advancement seemed scripted, echoing hollow promises. Following a set checklist of skills felt confining. I moved past the idea of fitting into a one-size-fits-all mold for success, realizing it wasn't about changing who I was fundamentally.

I embarked on a quest for answers, taking courses, diving into leadership literature, and studying insights from renowned experts. However, the more I delved, the clearer it became **true leadership isn't about ticking off skills or conforming to a formula**. While useful in initial stages, this approach couldn't capture what I admired in leaders – their authenticity and simplicity, which defied conventional rules.

The idea of pursuing a predefined list of skills fell short when aiming for higher, strategic roles. The leaders I admired hadn't risen by following a recipe or collecting credentials. There was something deeper at play, an elusive quality that set them apart. They embodied a genuine clarity in their leadership, an ease that couldn't be copied.

This chapter aims to uncover the nuances of leadership patterns, weaving together experiences, adaptability, and authenticity that I term "*EXECUTIVEness.*" It explores how our unique journeys shape the patterns we bring to leadership. As we delve into the link between our past and our approach to leadership, we'll uncover the seven mental patterns that shape our leadership mindsets.

2.1 Connecting the Threads of the Past

As I explored leadership patterns, I discovered a simple truth: our past experiences, values, culture, and more shape our leadership approach. Every challenge faced, every triumph, and each setback isn't isolated; they imprint patterns into our leadership style, leaving lasting marks.

Consider every obstacle, victory, and setback as pieces contributing to our understanding of leadership. These patterns aren't random; they reflect how we responded to pivotal moments. They stem from what we've learned, how we've evolved, and how we've grown from our experiences.

Let's be clear: it's not a passive shaping by the past; it's an active molding of our leadership style. This self-awareness and adaptability become guiding lights toward more effective leadership, resonating profoundly with top leaders.

Superior leadership isn't scripted by our past; it's a dynamic composition of experience, reflection, and intentional growth. The patterns we've developed aren't fixed destinies; they're building blocks that can be rearranged and refined. It's in this space of self-awareness and adaptive transformation that true excellence can thrive.

> OUR LEADERSHIP JOURNEY IS NOT A COLLECTION OF FRAGMENTED EXPERIENCES BUT A SYMPHONY OF GROWTH, RESILIENCE, AND INTENTIONAL DEVELOPMENT.

Let's now explore the connection between experience and pattern, gaining insight into how self-awareness and adaptation drive us forward.

2.2 Unveiling the Patterns

Think of leadership as a spectrum of expressions, not a rigid mold. The Leadership Mental Patterns capture diverse ways leadership brilliance emerges. These patterns include behaviors, inclinations, and approaches you bring to leadership. They're shaped not only by your history but also by your personality, beliefs, values, and experiences – influencing how you view leadership, its essence, and other leaders.

Imagine these patterns as reflections of your unique leadership journey. They encapsulate traits influenced by your triumphs, setbacks, and choices.

It's crucial to see these patterns as more than historical imprints; they mold your perception of challenges, guide team interactions, and influence how you pursue goals.

The Leadership Mental Patterns reveal your leadership philosophy, embodying who you are as a leader – a blend of innate qualities and journey imprints. Understanding and embracing these patterns provide insights for authentic leadership aligned with your true self.

This understanding challenges the notion that leadership is merely a checklist of skills or abilities. The fusion of these patterns shows leadership can't be distilled into formulas; it's about discovering and leveraging your unique pattern for effective leadership.

> THE LEADERSHIP MENTAL PATTERNS EMBODY THE LIVING ESSENCE OF OUR LEADERSHIP. THEY ARE THE CHEMISTRY OF OUR IDENTITY, BELIEFS, AND THE PECULIARITIES OF OUR INDIVIDUALITY AND OUR JOURNEY OF LEADERSHIP.

2.3 Unpacking the Patterns: Connections that Shape Your Leadership Mindset

EXECUTIVEness isn't about mastering technical skills; it's about the connections defining your leadership mindset. These connections bridge past experiences, present beliefs, and your leadership vision.

As we explore these complex connections, we uncover the essence of the 7 Leadership Mental Patterns – unique expressions of leadership brilliance that delve into the core of who you are.

1. **Governor Pattern**: If your journey emphasized adhering to rules and procedures, this pattern reflects your structured approach and focus on efficiency.

2. **Visionary Pattern**: Shaped by experiences valuing innovative thinking, this pattern drives you to envision new possibilities and lead change.

3. **Protector Pattern**: Rooted in fostering relationships, this pattern emphasizes collaboration, mentorship, and emotional support.

4. **Political Socialite Pattern**: Influenced by networking experiences, this pattern leverages relationships and social capital to achieve goals.

5. **Equilibrist Pattern**: Developed through navigating complexity, this pattern excels in balancing diverse perspectives and mediating conflicts.

6. **Enthusiast Pattern**: Fueled by initiative-taking engagement, this pattern energizes teams and confronts challenges with enthusiasm.

7. **Anti-hero Pattern**: Grounded in strategic thinking, this pattern excels in critical analysis and behind-the-scenes decision-making.

These patterns reflect more than past experiences; they shape your evolving leadership philosophy. They're the echoes of your identity, beliefs, and the dynamic interplay between your essence and leadership journey.

> UNDERSTANDING HOW THESE 7 LEADERSHIP MENTAL PATTERNS SHAPE YOUR LEADERSHIP EMPOWERS YOU TO EMBRACE YOUR INDIVIDUAL STYLE AUTHENTICALLY. IT'S ABOUT RECOGNIZING YOUR STRENGTHS AND APPLYING THEM PURPOSEFULLY, NOT CONFORMING TO A MOLD.

2.4 Embracing EXECUTIVEness Through Patterns

Identifying your dominant pattern unlocks your leadership potential. It's about recognizing inherent inclinations rather than conforming to a mold. These patterns fuse technical skills and emotional awareness, defining your leadership prowess.

Understanding and embracing your mental pattern reveals your authentic leadership style. These patterns guide interactions, decisions, and strategies dynamically, instead of fitting into a one-size-fits-all leadership model.

2.5 Translating EXECUTIVEness into Action: The Leadership Mental Patterns

Exercise: Pattern Self-Awareness Exercise

Step 1: Reflect on Your Pattern

- Find a quiet space for introspection.
- Recall your pattern attributes and how they align with leadership behaviors.

Step 2: Acknowledge Strengths and Positive Manifestations

- Note three ways your pattern strengths influence leadership positively.
- Reflect on building relationships, problem-solving, or achieving goals.

Step 3: Identify Challenges and Potential Drawbacks

- List challenges linked to your pattern-driven behaviors.

- Reflect on situations where behaviors might cause conflicts or hinder progress.

Step 4: Foster Personal Growth and Adaptation

- Plan how to enhance leadership effectiveness using pattern strengths.
- Strategize managing challenges linked to your pattern.

Step 5: Cultivate Awareness

- Document insights and apply self-awareness in leadership.
- Revisit periodically, adjusting strategies with evolving self-awareness.

Exercise: Pattern Observation Challenge

- Observe team behaviors for patterns resembling discussed leadership types.
- Note how past experiences influence their leadership approach.
- Engage in open discussions about experiences shaping their leadership.

Understanding and mastering the application of mental and leadership patterns is crucial for success. By recognizing and leveraging these patterns, you can navigate complex situations with confidence and effectiveness.

For more insights on the 7 Leadership Patterns and how they can transform your leadership approach, visit patrojas.com. There, you can learn about the test and how to get a free copy of "The 7 Leadership Mental Patterns" book.

Chapter 3:

The Art of Decision Making: Strategy Meets Emotion Enhancing through Strategy and Emotional Intelligence

In the previous chapter, we delved into the way our past experiences and the distinctive patterns we've woven together form our individual leadership view. With these unique leadership patterns now at the forefront of your understanding, let's dive headfirst into a fundamental aspect of leadership: the art of decision-making.

Decisions, as I've come to realize, resonate like ripples across teams and entire organizations, just like stones creating concentric circles in a tranquil pond. Yet, here's the fascinating part: decision-making isn't a standardized process that fits every scenario. It's a dynamic that involves thoughts, emotions, and the intriguing mental patterns we've been uncovering.

3.1 Balancing Rationality and Emotion in Decision-Making: Harmonizing Logic and Feeling

To illustrate this, let me begin with a real-life story that reveals a profound link between our logical decisions and the emotional currents beneath the surface.

Rationality x Emotion, the right approach:

Picture this: I found myself at the helm of an administrative team, the unsung heroes behind the scenes ensuring the smooth operation of everything. A team with exceptional skills, yet an enigmatic aspect colored our narrative. While we managed to keep attrition rates in check, the team's morale was plummeting. The vibrant energy was slipping away. Something was awry, prompting me to embark on a journey of discovery.

What captivated my attention was that our task appeared straightforward. We were on the hunt for individuals who excelled in the Microsoft suite, had a knack for numbers, and possessed a diligence that rivaled even the most meticulous auditors. These qualities were undeniably valuable. However, there was a twist in the tale.

Our team provided crucial support to our sales squad—a group fueled by emotions. It was a memo we had missed—the potency of these interpersonal connections and how they could sway outcomes. Our focus was on data, processes, and ticking off items on the to-do list. But what we had overlooked was the intangible essence of emotions—the secret ingredient behind our sales team's remarkable successes. This realization hit home.

And then, the epiphany arrived. It became evident that this wasn't solely about spreadsheets and task lists. It was about attuning to the rhythm of the sales team, understanding their needs, and grasping the hidden interplay of diverse leadership styles.

Here's what we uncovered: we had a mix of Visionary and Equilibrist leaders—trailblazers and stabilizers. While their attributes were invaluable, the emotional dimension had slipped through the cracks.

In response, we hit the pause button and embarked on a strategic recalibration. We fine-tuned our hiring criteria, seeking individuals who could thrive amidst high-pressure scenarios, adept at navigating the emotional rollercoaster that often accompanies sales organizations. Our training programs underwent a transformation too, shining a spotlight on the human component. We didn't just coach our team members on number-crunching; we empowered them to forge genuine human connections.

And that's when the magic happened. With team members attuned to the ebb and flow of emotions, we found our rhythm. We began to perceive that decisions rooted solely in technical prowess were only half of the equation. The other half encompassed a profound understanding of how emotions intertwine with every action and choice we make.

LEADERSHIP IS MORE THAN A MERE FORMULA. IT'S THE DYNAMIC BETWEEN LOGIC AND EMOTION. BECAUSE AT ITS CORE, BUSINESS IS ABOUT HUMAN INTERACTIONS, AND TRUE TRIUMPH ARISES FROM THAT VERY INTERSECTION.

3.2 The Dynamics of The Leadership Mental Patterns in Decisions

Let me illustrate how the distinctive leadership patterns we unveiled earlier can serve as a guide for your decision-making. Each pattern brings its unique strengths and potential pitfalls when it comes to pivotal choices. As we explore these patterns, remember that decisions transcend the simple binaries of right and wrong.

1. *Governor Pattern in Decisions: Governors, who rely on established procedures and rules, foster consistency, and*

predictability in decision-making. However, I've discovered that what may seem like stifling innovation in one context could be an essential anchor in another. Think of a visionary team member driven by creativity but prone to overlooking rules. In such cases, a leader patterned after the Governor can provide the structure needed to channel creativity productively.

2. ***Visionary Pattern in Decisions:*** *My observations reveal that Visionaries, propelled by innovation and risk-taking, lead groundbreaking decisions. Yet, I've learned that balancing visionary thinking with practical considerations is crucial. The key is combining visionary zeal with a dose of realism. This approach maintains the spark of innovation in decisions while grounding them in feasibility.*

3. ***Protector Pattern in Decisions:*** *Protector leaders, emphasizing collaboration and relationships, excel in harmonizing team dynamics through their choices. However, I've realized the importance of avoiding the postponement of tough decisions for the sake of harmony. It's about striking the right balance—nurturing relationships while making timely, strategic choices that foster team growth.*

4. ***Political Socialite Pattern in Decisions:*** *Political Socialite leaders thrive in networking and influence, yet I've come to see that an overemphasis on popular opinion can divert decisions from long-term goals. A balanced approach, integrating input with strategic thinking, resonates with both your team and organizational objectives.*

5. ***Equilibrist Pattern in Decisions:*** *Equilibrists, known for their balancing and strategizing, can sometimes overthink,*

resulting in decision paralysis. The key here is leveraging analytical abilities without falling into over-analysis. This way, decisions stem from both logical consideration and inherent equilibrium.

6. ***Enthusiast Pattern in Decisions:*** *I've noticed that enthusiastic leaders, fueled by fearlessness, often confront challenges head-on. Yet, a touch of assessment might be missing, glossing over potential risks. By channeling enthusiasm while ensuring comprehensive evaluation, decisions become informed and courageous.*

7. ***Anti-hero Pattern in Decisions****: The Anti-hero pattern involves a strategic approach shaped by careful analysis and a preference for working behind the scenes. Leaders embodying this pattern are more reserved and tend to prioritize observing and understanding complex situations before taking action. This pattern doesn't seek the spotlight; rather, it prefers to make an impact through thoughtful strategy. For Anti-heroes, decisions are not about personal recognition, but about achieving optimal outcomes for the team and the organization. Balancing their analytical prowess with calculated risk-taking, this pattern excels at navigating uncharted territories while avoiding unnecessary y exposure.*

Each of these patterns hold a multitude of possibilities, neither inherently good nor bad. It's the discernment we cultivate, understanding when to amplify or temper these traits, which transforms patterns into tools. Let's dig deeper, not just identifying patterns but using them to harness the full out potential in the decision-making process.

3.3 Exercises for Unveiling Your Decision-Making Patterns

The true potency of capability to make sound decisions lies in recognizing and applying our unique leadership patterns. Through these activities, you'll gain insights into how your pattern influences your choices, empowering you to make decisions aligned with your authentic leadership style.

Exercise: The Reflection Diary

This exercise will encourage you to reflect on your recent decisions and identify any recurring patterns in your approach.

- Set aside time at the end of each day to reflect on the decisions you've made.

- In a diary or journal, jot down the decisions you made and the thought processes behind them.

- Look for common themes or tendencies in your decision-making. Do you often prioritize practicality? Are you naturally drawn to innovative solutions? Do you tend to consider the impact on relationships?

- Reflect on how your leadership pattern might have influenced each decision. Did you lean toward the strengths of your pattern, or did you consciously adapt your approach?

Over time, you'll notice recurring patterns that align with your leadership style. This exercise will provide clarity on how your pattern influences your decision-making and where you might want to fine-tune your approach.

Exercise: Pattern Swap

This exercise involves stepping into the shoes of another pattern to gain a fresh perspective on decision-making.

- Choose a leadership pattern different from your own. It could be one you're less familiar with or one you'd like to explore.

- Imagine a recent decision you've made and view it from the perspective of the chosen pattern. How would a leader with that pattern approach the same decision?

- Consider the factors they might prioritize, the questions they might ask, and the potential outcomes they'd aim for.

- Reflect on the insights gained from this exercise. Did adopting a different pattern's perspective reveal new dimensions in your decision-making process?

By experiencing decision-making through the lens of another pattern, you'll expand your understanding of different approaches. This exercise fosters flexibility and adaptability in your decision-making repertoire.

Exercise: The Pattern Analyzer

This exercise will help you analyze a past decision in-depth to uncover the nuances of your pattern's influence.

Choose a crucial decision you've made recently. It could be related to your personal or professional life.

Break down the decision-making process: What were the factors you considered? How did you weigh the pros and cons? What emotions were present during the decision-making?

Now, analyze how your pattern played a role in each step of the way. Did it guide your priorities? Did it influence your perception of risks and rewards?

Reflect on the outcome of the decision. How did your pattern's influence shape the result?

This exercise offers a deep dive into how your pattern impacts the layers of decision-making. It unveils insights into your subconscious tendencies and provides a foundation for conscious decision-making alignment.

Through these exercises, you'll gain a holistic understanding of how your unique leadership pattern shapes your decision-making landscape. Armed with this knowledge, you'll be equipped to make decisions that resonate with your inherent style, with authenticity and impact.

3.4 Navigating the Challenges of Biased Decision-Making

As we dive deeper into decision-making, biases often seep into our choices, subtly distorting outcomes. In my quest to refine decision-making skills, I've realized that biases aren't mysterious enigmas or mere misconceptions. They're outcomes of the relationship between past experiences, inner tendencies, and external circumstances. These circumstances encompass the precise decision context—the timing, audience, purpose, and other variables subtly shaping our judgment.

> BIASES AREN'T RIGID BARRIERS. THEY'RE NOT
> UNCONTROLLABLE FORCES. THEY ARE MALLEABLE,
> MOLDED BY A RANGE OF INFLUENCES. THIS
> KNOWLEDGE ALLOWS US TO DISSECT AND
> UNDERSTAND THEIR ORIGINS AND DETECT THEIR
> PRESENCE BEFORE DECISIONS ARE MADE.

By acknowledging that biases aren't unexplainable mysteries, but discernible trends opens doors to comprehending our decision-making processes, you now can spot and understand how external factors or individual experiences influence your judgment.

Understanding biases as products of forces and circumstances grants you power to anticipate their effects. You can examine the context, analyze your reactions, and thoughtfully distance yourself from initial inclinations to make informed choices.

For instance, consider a scenario. Presented with two project proposals—one during an energized team meeting, the other in a casual setting—the first might sway you due to its enthusiasm, though the second idea could be more practical. Biases awareness is invaluable. You pause, acknowledge potential bias from the context, and assess the ideas impartially.

Demystify biases and understand them as outcomes of circumstances and influences. With this comprehension, you move through the process armed with clarity and wisdom, ensuring decisions are grounded in clear judgment and informed choice.

3.5 Translating *EXECUTIVEness* into Action: Decision Making Process

It's time to bridge the gap between knowledge and action. You've discovered leadership patterns and their influence on decisions.

However, knowledge alone is insufficient; it's application that truly counts.

Next, I propose practical scenarios and engaged reflections. Through these exercises, you'll experience firsthand how patterns harmonize, working in unison for successful decision-making.

Pattern Practice:

Delve into tailored case studies for each leadership pattern. Place yourself in the shoes of pattern-oriented leaders, dissecting their choices and impact. This exercise illuminates the interplay between your pattern and decision-making.

Decision Dialogues:

Engage in simulated dialogues with decisions mirroring real-world challenges. Embrace your pattern's perspective, balance its strengths, and acknowledge potential drawbacks. This fosters a pragmatic understanding of applying your pattern's wisdom.

Reflective Journaling:

After each exercise, record your thoughts. Your personal space to document insights, challenges, and "aha" moments. Over time, this journal evolves into a trove of self-awareness and growth.

> THE TOOLS YOU'VE COLLECTED AREN'T JUST ORNAMENTS FOR YOUR LEADERSHIP TOOLKIT; THEY ARE INSTRUMENTS THAT, WHEN MASTERFULLY WIELDED, ORCHESTRATE ASTOUNDING DECISIONS.

In the next chapter, you'll explore empathy and emotional understanding—pillars anchoring effective leadership's core. As you reflect on your growth, remember that equipping yourself with insights and tools empowers you to shape a powerful, personalized leadership style.

reflect on your growth, remember that equipping yourself with insights and tools empowers you to shape a powerful, personalized leadership style.

Chapter 4:

Empathy and Connection: Heartbeat of Authenticity - Unveiling Genuine Connections within Relationships

Welcome to a journey that dives deep into the heart of authentic leadership: Empathy and Connection. In today's fast-paced business world, empathy often gets tossed around as a buzzword, linked to vague notions of understanding and warm feelings. But let's set the record straight from the get-go. Empathy isn't just about nodding along or offering sympathy; it's a game-changing tool that empowers leaders to bridge gaps, elevate team dynamics, and achieve tangible results.

To understand empathy, we need to go beyond the surface. It's more than just feeling for others; it's about deeply connecting on cognitive, emotional, and compassionate levels. Throughout this chapter, we'll unpack what empathy really means in leadership—how it transforms cultures, fosters inclusivity, and builds authentic relationships.

Before you dive into empathy, it's important to recognize that this journey starts from within. Developing empathy requires more than just a superficial understanding – it requires a daily dedication to self-reflection, self-awareness, and truly connecting with our own emotions. In your leadership role, it's crucial for you to foster empathy within yourself, refining your ability to navigate the range of emotions and responses that leadership situations can trigger.

> WHEN YOU BECOME GROUNDED, EMOTIONALLY INTELLIGENT, AND IN COMMAND OF YOUR RESPONSES, YOUR AUTHENTICITY EMERGES AS A CRITICAL FORCE.

As leaders who lead with empathy, you should wield the extraordinary ability to cultivate a culture of understanding and compassion within your organization. This transformation isn't merely about implementing policies or initiatives; it's about weaving empathy into the very fabric of how you communicate, interact, and collaborate. By placing empathy at the forefront, you will nurture an environment where every voice is valued, where diverse viewpoints are embraced, and where trust takes root.

Empathy-infused leadership promotes open and honest dialogues, fosters inclusivity, and nurtures a sense of belonging. It empowers team members to share their thoughts, voice their concerns, and contribute their distinct perspectives. The cultural shift instigated by empathy transcends departmental divides, dissolves hierarchical barriers, and fosters a profound sense of unity among team members.

Get ready to explore practical strategies and real-life examples that highlight empathy's power in action. From creating supportive work environments to enhancing collaboration, empathy isn't just a soft skill—it's the driving force behind impactful leadership.

4.1 Unveiling the Essence of Empathy: Dispelling Misconceptions

Empathy is a multi-dimensional concept that goes beyond the surface; it encompasses cognitive, emotional, and compassionate dimensions. It's more than nodding along or using the right words.

Carol's Misconception:

Carol, a project manager, notices her team member Dave's unusual quietness and disengagement during meetings. Carol, aiming to be empathetic, approaches Dave and says, "I can see something's bothering you. Don't worry, everything will be fine!" It sounds compassionate, right? But here's the thing: Carol's words may be well-intentioned, but they miss the core of empathy.

In other occasions, Carol attempted to show her empathy by siding with her team or individual team members, with negative results.

Carol had a tough time grasping the concept of Empathy. And that is what we set to correct first!

4.2 The Influence of Empathy in Leadership

Empathy isn't just a soft skill; it's a strategic powerhouse that can reshape leadership. But how does it transition from an abstract idea to tangible results in the professional scope? This section uncovers the concrete benefits of empathy in leadership. Through real scenarios and measurable impacts, you'll see how empathy acts as a catalyst for positive change.

A transformative scenario:

Consider a real-life scenario where empathy played a pivotal role in transforming a team's dynamics.

Let's revisit the administrative team that supported the sales squad in the same space. This administrative team faced low engagement and growing dissatisfaction due to minor issues - interruptions from sales agents and the constant noise from their bustling counterparts.

Recognizing that addressing surface-level irritations wasn't enough, I encouraged the team to understand the underlying concerns. Through active listening, it became clear that visits from the sales team went beyond interruptions; they felt overwhelmed and cornered by their assertive presence. These interactions felt invasive and intimidating, leading to pressure and unease.

Pooling insights, a strategic solution emerged. We established a structured communication channel, funneling questions through supervisors to reduce direct contact and alleviate pressure. This simple adjustment not only minimized disruptions but also restored autonomy and respect for the administrative team.

Even the vibrant music favored by the sales team, which created a distracting cacophony for the administrative members, turned into an issue. Through empathy-driven discussions, a compromise was reached: specific time slots for music were established, balancing the needs of both teams.

What seemed like minor changes rooted in empathy yielded remarkable results. Administrative team engagement rose, absenteeism decreased, and overall productivity increased significantly. By addressing emotional undercurrents with empathy, we not only resolved issues but also fostered a more harmonious work environment.

This example showcases empathy's transformative influence on leadership dynamics. It's about recognizing emotional threads within an organization and using them for meaningful change. Empathy becomes a strategic tool, enabling leaders to grasp their teams' pulse, proactively address concerns, and drive tangible improvements.

> REMEMBER, EMPATHY ISN'T A BUZZWORD; IT'S AN ACTIONABLE FORCE THAT DRIVES AUTHENTIC AND IMPACTFUL ENGAGEMENT.

4.3 The Nexus of Empathy-Driven Decision-Making: How Empathy Shapes Choices

As a mentor to emerging leaders, I've witnessed the profound impact of empathy on decision-making. This section delves into the intricate relationship between empathy and leaders' choices, demonstrating how this fusion transforms outcomes into resonant successes. Let me share with you a tangible example that highlights the power of empathy-driven decision-making.

A mentee's journey: the impact of empathy on leadership:

Let me introduce you to Daniel, one of my mentees who navigated a challenging phase as a team leader.

His team faced consistent target misses, resulting in frustration and diminishing motivation. During our mentoring sessions, Daniel initially leaned toward a strict approach – imposing measures, reprimanding underperformers, and wielding authority. However, our discussions led us down a different path, one that hinged on empathy's power to transform.

Through probing questions, we unraveled the underlying issues behind the team's struggles. As Daniel engaged in one-on-one conversations with team members, he discovered an array of personal and professional challenges. Health concerns, family issues, and role ambiguities were unseeingly impacting the team's performance.

Empowered by his newfound insight into his team's predicaments, Daniel initiated open dialogues that encouraged team members to share their challenges. This transparent communication unveiled hidden obstacles and cultivated unity and a shared sense of purpose.

With empathy as the foundation, Daniel collaboratively crafted solutions that acknowledged individual circumstances while aligning with collective goals. As a result, team morale skyrocketed, and performance metrics steadily climbed.

By prioritizing empathy over coercion, Daniel transformed a struggling team into a harmonious unit that consistently surpassed expectations. This journey stands as a testament to empathy's profound influence on leadership and its potential to ignite positive change.

4.4 Empathy's Influence on Decision-Making: A Comprehensive View

I came to understand that empathy doesn't merely soften the edges of decision-making; it fortifies choices with a profound comprehension of the human elements at play. When leaders like Daniel infuse empathy into their decision-making processes, the effects reverberate throughout the organization. Decisions cease to be abstract directives; they become resonant selections that recognize individual realities, foster connections, and propel collective advancement.

But let's be clear, empathy-driven decisions are far from compromising standards or relinquishing goals. Instead, they elevate leadership to a level where choices are guided by a multifaceted awareness of both the task at hand and the individuals executing it. As demonstrated in Daniel's journey, the positive outcomes highlight that empathy-fueled choices not only lead to success but also cultivate growth, unity, and authentic satisfaction.

> EMPATHY-INFUSED CHOICES SHAPE THE NARRATIVE OF LEADERSHIP; THEY CRAFT A NARRATIVE OF HUMAN CONNECTION AND ACHIEVEMENT.

Here are key takeaways regarding the importance of empathy in decision-making processes:

1. **Understanding Before Deciding**: Empathy allows leaders to grasp the emotional and practical implications of decisions on individuals and teams.

2. **Building Trust and Alignment**: By considering diverse perspectives and emotions, empathy fosters trust and alignment within the organization.

3. **Enhancing Problem-Solving**: Empathy-driven decisions often lead to more creative and inclusive problem-solving approaches.

4. **Mitigating Risks of Miscommunication**: Effective empathy reduces the risks of misunderstandings and promotes clearer communication of decisions.

5. **Driving Sustainable Results**: Decision-making infused with empathy tends to yield sustainable and positive outcomes for both individuals and the organization.

4.5 Cultivating Empathy in Leadership: Nurturing a Culture of Understanding

I understand that empathy might not be inherent in everyone, yet it's entirely possible to cultivate. As leaders, nurturing empathy extends beyond personal development. It involves adopting a culture where empathy stands as a cornerstone, creating an environment where compassion and understanding flourish, leading to fortified bonds and enhanced team dynamics.

Leading with empathy is more than an ambitious goal; it's a pragmatic approach yielding tangible results. As a Superior Leader, it's important to recognize that team members are more than just cogs in a machine; they're individuals with unique stories, challenges, and aspirations. Acknowledging and empathizing with these aspects allows you to build a bridge of trust that transforms the workplace into a space where people feel valued and heard.

Here are three proven strategies for Cultivating Empathy:

- **Active Listening**: Foster active listening within your organization. Genuine listening deepens understanding and resolves conflicts more successfully.

- **Open Feedback Loop:** Establish an open feedback loop where team members can voice thoughts and concerns without fear. This nurtures a climate of transparency and trust.

- **Cross-Functional Collaboration:** Promote cross-functional collaboration to expose team members to diverse viewpoints, fostering a broader perspective.

Cultivating empathy within a team generates a ripple effect that extends beyond immediate interactions. Team members who experience empathy firsthand are more likely to extend it in their dealings with colleagues, clients, and even in their personal lives. This ripple effect strengthens relationships and bolsters overall organizational cohesion.

> WHILE EMPATHY IS OFTEN CATEGORIZED AS A SOFT SKILL, ITS IMPACT IS BOTH QUANTITATIVE AND QUALITATIVE.

An empathetic culture reduces turnover rates by cultivating a positive work environment. It stimulates creativity and innovation, as team members are more likely to share ideas without fear. Furthermore, empathy enhances collaboration, leading to efficient problem-solving and project execution.

4.6 Empathy in Action: A Transformative Scenario

The strategies outlined here are not just theoretical concepts; they are practical and actionable steps that can transform your leadership approach. As you start to work on nurturing empathy within your team, consider the words of Nick Wells, former mentee, now dear friend and collaborator, a seasoned executive who has successfully implemented these strategies:

"Active listening and fostering an open feedback loop have been game-changers for our team. By creating a space where every voice is heard and valued, we've seen a remarkable shift in collaboration and trust."

Nick's experience underscores the profound impact of empathy-driven practices.

When the odds are against you:

Picture a scenario where your team is suddenly entrusted with a high-stakes project and faces mounting pressure. Imagine encountering unforeseen obstacles that disrupt the already challenging plan.

Picture not being able to adhere to the budget or timeline, and envision working against overwhelming odds, facing failure before the project even takes off.

This isn't a mere hypothetical; this was a real scenario some of my direct reports once encountered.

Effective leader must reevaluate resources, timelines and support needed for the project to succeed. But effective empathetic leaders go further; they acknowledge the team's stress and take proactive steps to alleviate the burden. They listen to the team's concerns, strategize with them, provide more than expected resources, establish a sound flexible timeline, ensure a healthier workspace, and make themselves available.

This empathetic approach doesn't just boost team morale; it directly influences the project's success, underscoring the tangible benefits of empathy-driven leadership.

Remember, cultivating empathy is a continuous journey, one that transforms not only your leadership style but also the very essence of your organization's culture.

4.7 The Limits of Empathy: Balancing Empathy and Objectivity

While empathy is a potent tool, it's crucial to understand its limits and even recognize when excessive empathy might hinder objective decision-making… because sometimes it does. Striking a balance between understanding and impartiality is key, so let's talk about that.

Empathy often demands an emotional investment in grasping others' perspectives, emotions, and needs. However, excessive emotional involvement can cloud judgment and impede clear decision-making in certain situations. You must acknowledge this empathy-objectivity dilemma and navigate it with precision.

Take the story of Vicky, a team leader who initially struggled to balance empathy with objectivity due to personal challenges:

Balancing Empathy and Objectivity:

Vicky, a resolute team leader, faced significant personal and family challenges that heightened her empathy towards her team members. She empathized deeply with their individual struggles, often prioritizing their well-being over team performance metrics. While her compassion fostered a supportive work environment, it also inadvertently led to leniency and a lack of assertiveness when addressing underperformance or missed deadlines.

As deadlines approached and productivity lagged, Vicky's team began to experience setbacks. Despite her best intentions, her inability to strike a balance between understanding her team's challenges and maintaining performance standards hindered overall productivity. Colleagues and supervisors began to notice a pattern where empathy, while valued, sometimes compromised the team's ability to meet goals effectively.

Frustrated with her team's performance, realizing she needed a shift in approach, Vicky sought my mentorship to develop a more balanced leadership style. Through guidance and self-reflection, she learned to channel her empathy into constructive support while also setting clear expectations and boundaries. By promoting open communication and providing targeted assistance where needed, Vicky found a way to support her team's well-being without sacrificing performance standards.

If anything, please recognize the importance of maintaining a delicate equilibrium between empathy and objectivity in leadership. While empathy is a valuable asset for understanding and supporting team members, leaders must also exercise assertiveness and uphold organizational goals to ensure sustained success. The challenge lies in maintaining a delicate equilibrium between empathy and objectivity.

> EMPATHY SHOULDN'T DETER YOU FROM MAKING TOUGH DECISIONS WHEN NECESSARY. INSTEAD, IT SHOULD GUIDE YOU IN COMMUNICATING THOSE DECISIONS WITH SENSITIVITY AND TRANSPARENCY.

By striking this balance, you create an environment where empathy and objectivity coexist harmoniously.

When attempting to strike the Empathy-Objectivity Balance, consider:

- **Clear Communication:** Transparently communicating decisions and the rationale behind them. This ensures that while empathy is considered, objective factors are also acknowledged.

- **Structured Decision-Making:** Employing decision-making strategies that encompass both emotional and factual aspects. This prevents impulsive decisions driven solely by empathy.

In exercising *EXECUTIVEness*, the purpose of empathy is to serve as the lens through which objectivity is filtered. As a Superior Leader leverage your understanding of emotions to make informed decisions that account for the human impact. This approach doesn't negate objectivity but augments it with compassion and humanity.

Empathy is a guiding force, not a dictatorial rule. Empathy should guide you in comprehending diverse viewpoints, anticipating emotional reactions, and cultivating a supportive work environment. However, it shouldn't dictate decisions absolutely. The key lies in integrating empathy as a pivotal dimension of your decision-making toolkit.

> UNDERSTANDING THE BOUNDARIES OF EMPATHY IS AS CRITICAL AS CULTIVATING IT.

Recognizing the true form of empathy at work is just the beginning. The real impact comes from applying it thoughtfully and effectively. Embrace empathy not just as a concept, but as an actionable strategy that enhances every decision you make.

4.8 Translating *EXECUTIVEness* into Action: Cultivating Empathy

Empathy, like any skill, can be honed and fortified over time. Here I present you a few pragmatic exercises and reflections to aid in developing and enhancing empathetic skills. By participating in these activities, you will not only elevate your ability to connect deeply with team members but also contribute to fostering an atmosphere of genuine understanding and unwavering support.

Reflection: The Ripple Effect

- Recall a time when someone showed genuine empathy during a challenging situation. How did their empathy impact your perception and feelings about the situation?

- Consider how you can create a similar ripple effect within your team or organization. Reflect on how your empathetic actions can positively influence others' emotional well-being and contribute to a supportive work environment.

Reflection: Empathy's Impact on Decision-Making

- Recollect a recent decision-making situation involving multiple stakeholders. Reflect on how empathy influenced your approach to the decision.

- Did considering others' perspectives lead to a more inclusive decision? How did empathy help anticipate potential emotional responses and improve the overall outcome?

Exercise: The Empathy Challenge

- Choose a colleague and engage in a conversation focused solely on understanding their perspective. Refrain from offering advice or sharing your own experiences unless explicitly asked.

- Practice active listening by asking open-ended questions and creating a safe space for them to express themselves. Reflect on how this exercise enhances your empathetic skills and deepens your connection with your colleagues.

Reflection: The Unseen Impact

- Think about instances where you've practiced empathy without immediate visible outcomes. For example, supporting a team member through a personal challenge or demonstrating patience during a difficult project.

- Reflect on how these empathetic actions contribute to fostering an empathy-driven culture within your team or organization over time.

> CULTIVATING EMPATHY IS A CONTINUOUS JOURNEY, REQUIRING COMMITMENT, SELF-AWARENESS, AND A WILLINGNESS TO LEARN FROM EVERY INTERACTION. BY INFUSING EMPATHY, YOU'RE NOT ONLY SHAPING INDIVIDUAL LIVES BUT ALSO MOLDING A WORKPLACE WHERE COMPASSION AND UNDERSTANDING THRIVE.

Conclusion: Embracing Empathy as a Leadership Imperative

As we conclude, consider this: empathy isn't merely a soft skill but a transformative force that shapes cultures, nurtures collaboration, and drives organizational success. By cultivating empathy within ourselves and championing it within our teams, we open doors to deeper connections, innovative solutions, and resilient organizational dynamics.

Now, reflect on your own leadership journey. How can you integrate empathy more intentionally into your daily interactions and decision-making processes? How might fostering empathy empower your team members to thrive, contribute more authentically, and foster a culture of trust and understanding?

Remember that empathy begins with self-awareness and extends through active listening, compassionate decision-making, and fostering a supportive environment. Let empathy guide you in navigating challenges, inspiring others, and building a workplace where every voice is valued.

Empower your leadership with empathy. The ripple effects of understanding, compassion, and genuine connection will not only elevate your leadership but also enrich the lives of those you lead.

How will you embrace empathy in your leadership today?

Chapter 5:

Self-Awareness: Navigating Strengths and Growth - Elevated Understanding and Personal Growth

What drives *EXECUTIVEness?* This chapter is about something extremely elementary but profoundly impactful but generally misunderstood– self-awareness. In a landscape rich with elements like logic, emotional savvy, prowess and audacity, self-awareness stands as the linchpin. It's not the stuff of poetic narratives; it's the grit that fuels authentic leadership.

> SELF-AWARENESS ISN'T JUST A BUZZWORD; IT'S THE COMPASS IN THE CHAOS OF LEADERSHIP. IT'S WHAT GUIDES OUR DECISIONS, ACTIONS, AND INTERACTIONS. THINK OF IT AS YOUR NORTH STAR, ALWAYS KEEPING YOU ON TRACK.

So, let's dig in and turn the attention to you. Let's focus not just on your strengths and aspirations, but your blind spots and biases too. Because that's what it takes – a no-nonsense look at yourself – to truly grow as a *Superior Leader.*

This chapter is about getting your hands dirty, doing the work, and owning your growth. It's about stripping away the fluff and standing face-to-face with what makes you tick as a leader. Because here's the truth: mastering your leadership starts with mastering yourself. And that's what we're here to do.

5.1 The Mirror of Self-Assessment: Facing Your Strengths and Gaps

Alright, let's cut through the noise and get straight to the point – leadership isn't a one-size-fits-all deal. It's about understanding what makes you tick, what drives you, and where you stumble. This self-awareness isn't an elusive concept; it's the bedrock of *EXECUTIVEness.*

So, let's grab that mirror and take a good, hard look. We're not doing this to inflate egos or wallow in self-doubt. We're doing it to build a clear, unfiltered picture of your strengths and areas that need focus.

Understanding Your Strengths:

Self-awareness isn't about dwelling on weaknesses alone. It's about acknowledging where you shine. Maybe it's your ability to remain cool under pressure, or your ability to make like you, or your knack for seeing the bigger picture. These strengths are your toolkit, the reliable resources to strengthen your leadership skills. We're not just identifying them; we're celebrating them, because that's where your true power lies.

Unearthing Your Blind Spots:

Let's be real – we all have them. Blind spots are those tricky corners of our personality we often overlook, and they can trip us up if we're not careful. Maybe it's a tendency to micromanage, or wanting to always have the last word, or a reluctance to delegate.

These aren't character flaws; they're areas that need a bit of light shone on them. And that's what we're going to do – unearth those blind spots and bring them into focus.

Embracing Growth Areas:

Here's the thing – **self-awareness isn't about just acknowledging the gaps; it's about committing to growth.** If you're not the best communicator or struggle to trust your team fully, that's alright. Identifying these areas is the first step to transforming them into strengths. It's about saying, "Okay, this is where I need work, and I'm ready to put in the effort."

This isn't a cozy fireside chat; it's a no-nonsense exploration of who you are as a leader. We're not tiptoeing around your potential; we're diving headfirst into it. Because understanding your strengths and areas for growth is how you elevate your leadership game. It's not about aiming for perfection; it's about striving for progress. And that starts with the mirror in front of you.

5.2 The Power of Strengths: Unleashing Your Potential

Strengths aren't just fancy attributes to brag about; they're your unique weapons in the leadership battlefield.

This section isn't about fluff or vague self-affirmations; it's about identifying what you're really good at, and then using that knowledge to lead with purpose.

Discovering Your Unique Arsenal:

Let's start with strengths assessments. We're not talking about those superficial online quizzes that tell you what kind of pizza you'd be. This is about diving into the core of your leadership persona.

Why? Because your strengths define you in ways you might not realize. They're the qualities that set you apart and give you that extra edge. We're going to unravel your strengths – the ability to rally a team, your gift for strategic thinking, your knack for problem-solving. Once you know what you've got in your arsenal, you'll approach leadership challenges with more clarity and confidence.

Benefits of Unleashing Strengths:

Listen, knowing your strengths isn't about putting a feather in your cap; it's about being smart. We're talking about improving team dynamics, boosting productivity, and making strategic decisions that align with your natural abilities. I've seen leaders' step into their strengths, and the transformation is electric. You become the leader your team needs, and that's not just leadership; it's empowerment.

The Art of Progression:

Although it's tempting to bask in your strengths, but leadership isn't a one-trick pony show. It's about growth. This means it's time to address those growth areas. We all have them, those areas that might not be your forte, but they can't be ignored. Self-awareness is about seeing them and working on them. It's the difference between stagnation and progress.

Imagine a leader who recognized a growth area, tackled it head-on, and not only transformed that area but also gained a new perspective on leadership. This is where the rubber meets the road; it's about embracing the challenge and emerging stronger.

We're not building fairy tales here; we're building a roadmap to your best leadership self. It's about mastering your strengths and facing your growth areas – because that's how you propel forward.

> YOUR STRENGTHS AREN'T JUST ATTRIBUTES; THEY'RE THE FOUNDATION OF YOUR LEADERSHIP STORY. AND IT'S TIME TO MAKE THAT STORY LEGENDARY.

5.3 Illuminating Shadows: Confronting Weaknesses

Let's delve into a subject we often dodge – our weaknesses. Now, I'm not here to deliver an inspirational speech or tell you to don a cape of vulnerability. This is about something more substantial – understanding that **weaknesses aren't chinks in your armor, they're the raw materials for growth.**

Confronting your shadows and embracing imperfections is an integral aspect of leadership. Recognizing your own weaknesses isn't an invitation for self-criticism or garnering pity. Embracing your imperfections doesn't equate to surrendering; rather, it showcases your dedication to personal development and progress.

Transforming a weakness into a strength:

Take, for instance, a colleague in my sphere who had a habit of being overly critical. Nothing was never good enough for her. If there was an opportunity to find a flaw, she will take it, if there was none, she will create scenarios for it...

Instead of brushing it off as an inherent trait, we harnessed this inclination to benefit the organization. She became the designated devil's advocate during brainstorming sessions, using her critical perspective to push the team towards thorough analysis and initiative-taking problem-solving. What was once seen as a drawback quickly became a crucial asset, elevating the team's decision-making dynamic.

It's imperative to grasp that embracing weaknesses isn't indicative of inadequacy; rather, it serves as a signal of your firm dedication to achieving excellence.

Self-awareness functions as a compass, guiding you through uncharted territories and empowering you to metamorphose moments of doubt—those instances of "I'm not proficient"—into resounding accomplishments exclaiming, "Witness my mastery."

EMBRACING WEAKNESSES TRANSCENDS FIXATING ON THEM OR AFFORDING THEM UNDUE PROMINENCE. INSTEAD, IT INVOLVES A PROFOUND REALIZATION THAT YOUR LEADERSHIP EFFICACY IS ROOTED IN COMPREHENDING THE INTRICACIES OF YOUR COMPETENCIES.

As you confront these aspects that might be less illuminated, bear in mind that weaknesses don't confine you; rather, they present fertile ground for your transformation and renewal.

5.4 Translating *EXECUTIVEness* into Action: The Self-Aware Leader's Toolkit

Strategic self-awareness isn't an ethereal concept confined to leadership discussions; it's a pragmatic toolkit capable of elevating your leadership from good to exceptional. This section is about equipping you with tangible tools that can chisel your leadership persona into one that resonates with those you guide.

Exercise: Unveiling Core Values

Let's start with the foundation – your values. This isn't just an exercise in eloquence; it's about discovering what truly matters to you and how those values shape your decisions.

Here's the method: pick up a journal and dive in. Pen down your values, free from external pressures or clichés. Does integrity outweigh profit for you? Does collaboration overshadow competition?

As you explore your core values, you'll discover that they become your guiding North Star, shaping your leadership choices. Aligning actions with values isn't an unrealistic idea; it's a strategy that forges strong and determined leaders.

Reflection: Uncovering Patterns

Bias isn't a relic of the past; it's an ongoing hurdle we all confront. Concentrate on moments when recognizing biases influenced your leadership decisions. Did you pivot your direction? Did you mitigate the consequences? Sharing these insights isn't about baring vulnerabilities; it's about nurturing collective advancement.

As a leader, acknowledging unconscious biases is your passport to crafting more inclusive choices and cultivating a team that appreciates your transparency.

Exercise: Embracing the Growth Mindset Challenge

Growth isn't confined to your garden; it's a mindset that can reshape you. The challenge? Embrace a zone of growth. Perhaps it's public speaking, technology integration, or even embracing delegation. This isn't a plunge into the abyss; it's a measured stride into your growth territory.

A growth mindset doesn't render you failure-proof; it fortifies your resilience in its face.

Reflection: Sustaining Equilibrium

Consider your journey of self-awareness. The balance you've struck between strengths and areas for improvement isn't a final destination; it's a dynamic state. Contemplate how this equilibrium is shaping your approach to leadership. Are you leading with heightened assurance? Are you navigating challenges more adeptly? Balance doesn't entail constructing a sterile uniformity; it entails embracing the interplay of your facets and knowing their worth.

As explore your toolkit of the self-aware leader, remember that this is not a solo endeavor. It's a shared voyage of self-discovery and growth. Every exercise, every moment of reflection, isn't just about refining yourself; it's about magnifying your impact.

Chapter 6:

Adaptability and Resilience: Forging Strength - Harnessing Resilience and Flexibility in Challenges

Looking back on my journey to professional accomplishment, it's clear that life has been my greatest teacher. It didn't just teach me from books; it threw me into diverse cultures and unfamiliar situations, demanding adaptability and resilience at every turn. Among the myriad lessons etched into my core, none shine as brightly as the significance of adaptability and resilience.

In a world often bound by rigid norms, my journey resembled a mosaic of unexpected twists and turns. How many times did I find myself navigating the complexities of unfamiliar places, contexts, and cultures, feeling like a stranger among familiar faces? These moments of puzzling unfamiliarity evolved into my greatest strengths. Stripped of conventional biases, I learned to rely on my internal compass, interpreting situations through my unique lens shaped by life experiences.

True adaptability wasn't just an option for me – it became a necessity, a way of life. Each new encounter demanded recalibration of my perspective and approach, often requiring me to shed old assumptions, acknowledge vulnerability, and embrace the unknown.

This chapter examines the essence of adaptability and resilience, qualities that have been my steadfast companions throughout my journey. It offers insights and practical tools not just for surviving but thriving in the face of challenges and uncertainty. Through personal stories, transformative revelations, and actionable insights, I aim to equip you with the invaluable armor of adaptability and resilience.

6.1 Embracing Change: The Cornerstone of Adaptability

Change is constant in leadership—it's what keeps us on our toes and drives transformative impact in decision-making. It challenges our comfort zones, stretches our capabilities, and introduces us to the unknown. But adaptability isn't just about weathering these changes; it's about embracing them.

Embracing change is catalyzed by cultivating a global perspective– a lens that reveals the diversity of human experiences across different contexts and cultures. It's about recognizing that what is familiar to you isn't necessarily familiar to others, and vice versa. This perspective doesn't just broaden your worldview; it invites you to consider new perspectives, stretch your understanding, and contemplate fresh ideas.

When you consider, practice and adopt this global perspective magic happens. This mindset isn't just a concept; it's a powerful ally against stagnation, a driving force that propels you to see change not as a nuisance but as an opportunity for personal and professional growth. It encourages you to view challenges as steppingstones toward honing your capabilities.

Take, for instance, relocating to lead in a new country. Initially daunting, right? But with a global perspective, we start to appreciate and explore the nuances of our unfamiliar environment. You recognize that your leadership style might need to adapt to accommodate diverse cultural expectations. Here, the growth mindset guides you. Instead of being intimidated by this change, you approach it as a chance to learn and expand your leadership toolkit.

Adaptability - this aptitude thrives on informed, flexible, and agile decision-making, qualities that become second nature as you harness the power of a macro perspective and a growth mindset.

> WITH THIS ADAPTIVE ABILITY, CHANGE CEASES TO BE A FORCE TO ENDURE; RATHER, IT BECOMES A TIDE TO RIDE, CARRYING YOU TOWARD BROADER HORIZONS OF LEADERSHIP.

6.2 Resilience in Leadership: Navigating Storms

Resilience is not just about bouncing back from setbacks; it's about thriving despite them, even when the odds seem insurmountable. This section explores how resilience isn't a trait you're born with, but a skill set you cultivate and nurture over time. It's about learning from failures, adapting to new situations, and maintaining your balance in turbulent times.

Think of resilience as a muscle you strengthen with each challenge. When faced with adversity, it's your emotional awareness and logical thinking that keep you on track. This resilience isn't just personal—it sets the tone for your team's response to setbacks, fostering a culture where challenges are opportunities in disguise.

Resilience isn't a singular trait; it's a collection of skills and attitudes that empower you to bounce back from setbacks. It's the ability to recalibrate when faced with adversity, rather than being thrown off course. This resilience is essential for growth since it harnesses emotional awareness and logical ability to find the best path forward.

The development of resilience, much like a muscle, is a gradual growth that strengthens over time. It's illuminated by your ability to draw lessons from failures, to adapt to new situations, and to maintain your balance in the midst of turbulence. Here, your experiences of adapting to unfamiliar environments come into play, providing you with a multitude of tools to navigate through uncharted waters.

> THE POWER OF RESILIENCE IS FELT WHEN YOU REFUSE TO BE SUBDUED BY CHALLENGES. A SETBACK DOESN'T DEFINE YOU; IT'S MERELY AN ASPECT OF YOUR LEADERSHIP JOURNEY.

This mindset shift, fostered by your experiences of embracing change, further solidifies the link between adaptability and resilience.

Consider the demanding situation of leading a team through a sudden market downturn. You tap into your knowledge of global perspectives, enabling you to anticipate and plan for potential shifts. As the downturn hits, your growth mindset guides you to view this as an opportunity to optimize and restructure strategies.

Your resilience takes center stage as you communicate transparently with your team, acknowledging the challenges but steering them towards innovative solutions. In this way, adaptability and resilience emerge, showcasing how these two facets intertwine harmoniously.

I want to make it clear that adaptability and resilience are a must in the foundation of *EXECUTIVEness*. They amplify your impact, enabling you to not only make informed decisions but also to thrive in the face of adversity.

6.3 Thriving Amidst Uncertainty: Harnessing Adaptability

In leadership, as in life, uncertainty is a constant companion. It looms as market dynamics shift, technologies evolve, and unexpected challenges emerge. And it's amidst this uncertainty that your adaptability must shine. This section delves into the ways in which you can amplify your adaptability, allowing you to thrive through the ever-changing landscape.

> ADAPTABILITY IS NOT A PASSIVE SURRENDER TO CHANGE; IT'S A PROACTIVE ENGAGEMENT WITH IT.

It's the ability to pivot swiftly, capitalizing on new opportunities and responding to challenges with agility. Your experiences of embracing change, especially in diverse environments, forge a foundation of adaptability that must be firmly rooted in your leadership journey

Life isn't about smooth sailing; sometimes, you find yourself in uncharted waters. But guess what? That's where your true resolve shines – in the midst of uncertainty.

Stepping back to spring forward:

I initially pursued a career in sales despite lacking any prior experience. Sales wasn't exactly within my comfort zone, but I believed in the dream timeshare vacations offered, so I took the leap. Over three years, I ascended from a novice salesperson to a sales manager position. The journey was incredible. professionally and financially rewarding but strained my personal life. The demanding schedule, including weekends and holidays, meant missing precious moments with my daughter. Bella, at the time, was a toddler, still experiencing many of her firsts, and I wasn't there to share them with her. While I excelled professionally, my personal life suffered. It became clear that a change was needed to align my career with my personal goals.

With newfound purpose and clarity, I decided to look for a less unpredictable job, but something that allowed me to leverage all that knowledge I had acquired in that industry, so I ventured into the marketing side of timeshare, as a telemarketing sales agent. Some may have questioned this move, given the loss of benefits and great commissions, but I wasn't afraid to embrace the unknown. Time with my daughter and a balanced 9 to 5 lifestyle was more valuable than material rewards at that point.

Fast forward five years, and I've progressed from telemarketing agent to director of marketing. This role not only provided professional growth and benefits but also offered collaborative opportunities beyond what I ever imagined.

The fusion of mental prowess and emotional smarts played a pivotal role in my life. It armed me with the ability to make risky moves that aligned with my aspirations. It helped me see setbacks as steppingstones, guiding my path without losing sight of my goals.

And in here, I found myself on a thrilling new trajectory. Leading dynamic teams, driving exciting projects, and eventually becoming the Vice President of Strategic Marketing and Compliance at one of the world's top vacation companies.

But there's more to the story. My global escapades were like a masterclass in adaptability. New countries, cultures, languages – they taught me a thing or two. You see, adaptability isn't just a skill; it's a way of life.

Here's the bottom line: uncertainty isn't your adversary; it's your ally. It's a platform to display your resilience and your adaptability muscle, it's about embracing those detours and owning them. It's about making the most of life's surprises.

> ADAPTABILITY ISN'T JUST ABOUT SURVIVING THE STORM; IT'S ABOUT STEERING RIGHT INTO IT. IT'S ABOUT FACING YOUR FEARS, PUSHING LIMITS, AND KNOWING THAT WHILE THE DESTINATION IS IMPORTANT, THE JOURNEY ITSELF IS FULL OF INVALUABLE LESSONS AND GROWTH.

6.4 Resilience: The Art of Bouncing Back

Resilience stands as the cornerstone of enduring leadership—an unwavering spirit that propels you forward when challenges deliver their blows.

Resilience isn't about evading setbacks; it's about navigating them with unwavering resolve. Your experiences of embracing change, coupled with your adaptability, have forged the steel of resilience in your leadership approach. When faced with adversity, you don't crumble; you spring back, stronger, and wiser.

EXECUTIVEness lays the foundation for this resilience, endowing you with the mental agility to reframe setbacks as opportunities for growth. Instead of lingering on failures, you glean insights that fuel your future decisions. It's this fusion of cognitive acumen and emotional understanding that enables you to rise above difficulties, time and again.

Nothing describes this better than Suzanne's inspiring journey.

An embodiment of resilience in action:

Imagine a New York City native uprooting her life to embrace a new chapter in Florida. This move meant bidding farewell to a fulfilling decade-long career, leaving behind friends, and venturing into unfamiliar territory devoid of her established support network.

After seven months of job searching yielding no offers, Suzanne's spirit remained unbroken. Recognizing something needed to change, she reached out to me for guidance. This first step epitomized resilience in action—courageously seeking help and humbly embracing change.

Together, we crafted a strategic plan, involving Suzanne's self-rebranding and a deep reassessment of her aspirations. Our strategy involved setting sights on roles she might have once overlooked, culminating in her even interviewing for a non-managerial position. This step, though unconventional, embodied adaptability and a willingness to explore new avenues.

During that interview, less than three months into our collaboration, Suzanne's resilience, courage, and growth mindset captivated the interviewers and was offered a promotion and salary adjustment during the interview process. Their offer exceeded all expectations, not merely aligning with her interviewed role but surpassing her previous pay and position in New York City. This was an offer that not only acknowledged her value but also her potential… and the cherry on top? Working from home! It checked all her boxes and even more!

Suzanne's story illuminates the core of resilience—the ability to navigate challenges while remaining open to the opportunities they present. Resilience isn't about enduring storms; it's about seizing hidden opportunities, even those masquerading as setbacks, and emerging victorious. It's about acknowledging and seeking assistance; it's about being adaptable and resolute regardless of the hurdles in your path.

Resilience isn't solely an individual trait; it reverberates through your team's dynamics. Your leadership instills a culture of resilience, where setbacks are met not with blame but with collective problem-solving. This is where the brilliance emerges: it empowers you not only to nurture resilience within yourself but to sow its seeds in those you lead.

> THE SYNERGY BETWEEN RESILIENCE AND EXECUTIVENESS BECOMES EVIDENT AS YOU WITNESS YOUR TEAM NOT JUST RECOVERING FROM SETBACKS BUT HARNESSING THOSE EXPERIENCES TO PROPEL THEMSELVES FORWARD. IT'S A SHARED UNDERSTANDING THAT FAILURES ARE STEPPINGSTONES, NOT STUMBLING BLOCKS.

6.5 Translating *EXECUTIVEness* into Action: Cultivating Adaptability and Resilience

Adaptability and resilience transcend theoretical concepts; they are skills sharpened through purposeful practice. This section empowers you with tangible steps and introspective exercises to infuse these qualities into the very fabric of your leadership style.

Exercise: Embracing Change Mindfully

- Reflect on a recent situation where unexpected change swept through your path. Analyze your initial responses and subsequent actions.

- Explore the emotions that arose within you. Did they hinder your adaptability or steer it?

- Imagine how a more adaptable approach might have altered the outcome. Consider alternative reactions and decisions stemming from heightened adaptability.

Reflection: Learning from Setbacks

- Recall a past setback or challenge from your journey. Explore the emotions that influenced your response and trace the outcome's trajectory.

- Examine how resilience shaped your decisions. Did it spur growth, fuel innovation, or offer new perspectives?

- Consider how you can harness and magnify resilience in future challenges.

Exercise: Nurturing a Growth Mindset

- Spot a recent scenario where change was met with resistance. Walk the path of your initial thoughts and feelings as you navigated the unfamiliar.

- Evoke a unique perspective—one that welcomes growth and the unknown. Try to explore this landscape of possibilities.

- Live out this shift in mindset as you confront future challenges. Document any changes in your reactions, nurturing a growth-oriented outlook.

Reflection: Harnessing Personal Resilience

- Travel back to a moment where a significant personal or professional setback once took place. Reexamine the tools from your toolkit that aided your resurgence.

- Consider how the learnings and positives of that setback can be employed to fortify your resilience as you continue moving ahead.

Adaptability and resilience don't stand apart from the bedrock of *EXECUTIVEness* we've been cultivating; they are its inherent elements.

Chapter 7:

Mastering Communication: The Voice of Connection - Transparent and Impactful Interaction

In Superior Leadership, there's an undeniable force that fuels collaboration, drives change, and propels success – communication.

Communication isn't merely the transmission of messages; it's the craft of forging connections, fostering understanding, and nurturing relationships. In a landscape where information is abundant, yet clarity isn't guaranteed, mastering the art of communication is paramount.

This chapter is about understanding the intricate dynamics of human interaction, embracing communication as a strategic enabler and delving into practical tactics, real-world scenarios, and providing straightforward advice.

Consider this chapter your manual for refining the language of leadership – one that slices through the noise, establishes profound connections, and instigates meaningful change.

7.1 Active Listening: The Basis of Meaningful Communication

Communication isn't solely about articulating words; it's also about being a receptive and engaged listener. Active listening, often underestimated, is the base for meaningful communication that drives collaboration, fosters understanding, and strengthens relationships. It's not merely nodding in agreement or waiting for your turn to speak; it's a deliberate practice that involves fully immersing yourself in the speaker's words, thoughts, and emotions.

Active listening is about creating a safe and open space where the speaker feels valued and understood. This not only involves techniques such as taking notes to capture key points, asking open-ended questions to encourage deeper insights, and providing paraphrased feedback to confirm understanding, but most importantly, requires a truthful desire to understand and value what others have to say.

WHEN YOU PRACTICE ACTIVE LISTENING, YOU SUSPEND YOUR URGE TO FORMULATE RESPONSES WHILE THE SPEAKER IS TALKING. INSTEAD, YOU FOCUS ON DIGESTING THE MESSAGE, COMPREHENDING ITS NUANCES, AND RECOGNIZING THE EMOTIONS UNDERLYING THE WORDS. BY DOING SO, YOU DEMONSTRATE RESPECT AND EMPATHY, ENHANCING YOUR ABILITY TO RESPOND THOUGHTFULLY AND CONSTRUCTIVELY.

But as everything we discussed, there is a difference between understanding and embracing a concept and actually practicing it, and most fail in that area.

Active Listening is Not:

- **Selective Hearing:** Active listening isn't cherry-picking parts of the conversation that align with your preconceived notions. It involves being open to the entirety of the message, even if it challenges your perspective.

- **Interrupting:** Interrupting disrupts the speaker's flow and signals a lack of patience. Active listening entails giving the speaker space to express themselves fully before you respond.

- **Prejudgment:** Forming judgments before the speaker has finished speaking hinders active listening. It's essential to withhold assumptions and remain open to the speaker's complete message.

- **Thinking Ahead:** Active listening isn't about planning your response while the speaker talks. It's about immersing yourself in the present moment and absorbing the information being shared.

And its value? Active listening serves multifaceted purposes in communication:

- **Understanding:** It deepens your comprehension of the speaker's perspective, allowing you to see the topic from their point of view.

- **Empathy:** Active listening helps you grasp the speaker's emotions, enabling you to respond in a way that acknowledges their feelings.

- **Trust Building:** By demonstrating that you genuinely care about what's being said, you foster trust and strengthen relationships.

- **Problem-Solving:** Through active listening, you gather insights that aid in identifying solutions and addressing concerns accurately.

ACTIVE LISTENING ELEVATES YOUR COMMUNICATION TO A HIGHER LEVEL. IT'S THE FOUNDATION UPON WHICH COLLABORATION, MUTUAL RESPECT, AND MEANINGFUL DIALOGUE ARE BUILT, MAKING IT AN ESSENTIAL SKILL FOR EVERY ASPIRING LEADER.

7.2 Crafting Clear and Concise Messages: The Power of Simplicity

In an era flooded with information, the ability to distill complex concepts into clear, succinct messages is a skill that distinguishes impactful leaders.

Jargon, convoluted phrases, and excessive details can muddy the waters, leading to misunderstandings and missed opportunities… but how not to use them? We sound smart when we use them, right?

"We need to optimize our operational synergies through the implementation of strategic paradigm shifts" sounds much better than *"Let's improve how we work together for better results"*

Or

"We shouldn't attempt to boil the ocean; instead, lets focus on the bleeding edge, and optimizing our bandwidth to truly move the needle and achieve our goals" sounds more impactful than: *"Let's concentrate on what matters, cut the unnecessary stuff, stay innovative and use our resources wisely to make a real impact"*

But in truth, simplicity and clarity are the cornerstones of communication. The power of simplicity in presenting ideas in a manner that resonates with your audience while preserving their essence, in a way that anyone and everyone clearly understands the core message.

Crafting clear messages demands a thoughtful process of simplification without diluting its content. To harness the power of simplicity in your communication try to:

- **Prune the Verbiage:** Trim excess words that don't contribute to the message's essence. Use concise language that conveys meaning without unnecessary embellishments.

- **Eliminate Ambiguity:** Ambiguity breeds confusion. Be direct in your communication, leaving no room for misinterpretation.

- **Know Your Audience:** Tailor your message to your audience's familiarity with the subject matter. Adjust your language and level of detail accordingly.

- **Highlight Key Points:** Identify the key takeaways you want your audience to retain. Structure your message around these focal points.

- **Use Analogies:** Analogies simplify complex ideas by drawing parallels to familiar concepts. They enhance understanding and make your message relatable.

- **Practice Brevity:** A concise message captures attention and ensures your audience grasps the core idea quickly.

SIMPLICITY IN COMMUNICATION DOESN'T MEAN SACRIFICING DEPTH; IT MEANS ENHANCING ACCESSIBILITY. WHEN YOUR TEAM UNDERSTANDS YOUR MESSAGE CLEARLY, THEIR ALIGNMENT AND ENGAGEMENT AMPLIFY, DRIVING BETTER OUTCOMES.

7.3 Building Authentic Connections: The Human Element in Communication

Amid the digital age's noise, the essence of authentic communication stands as a firm pillar. Building authentic connections goes beyond conveying information; it's about fostering trust, empathy, and rapport that elevate your leadership.

Authentic communication stems from genuineness. It's about being sincere, open, and vulnerable when appropriate. Authenticity fosters a sense of belonging, where team members feel valued as individuals, not just roles.

To infuse authenticity into your communication, practice the following:

- **Be Present:** Engage fully during conversations. Show that you're invested in what's being discussed.

- **Listen Actively:** Give undivided attention, understand perspectives, and respond thoughtfully.

- **Share Personal Insights:** Appropriately share experiences and stories that connect on a human level.

- **Admit Imperfections:** Embrace vulnerability by acknowledging mistakes and demonstrating a commitment to improvement.

- **Empathize:** Understand and acknowledge others' emotions, displaying your concern for their well-being.

- **Align Words and Actions:** Consistency between what you say and what you do reinforces trust.

> AUTHENTIC COMMUNICATION STRENGTHENS RELATIONSHIPS AND ENCOURAGES OPEN DIALOGUE. IT'S A CATALYST FOR COLLABORATION AND A CORNERSTONE FOR SUPERIOR LEADERSHIP.

By building connections rooted in authenticity, you foster an environment where communication transcends transaction, becoming a conduit for meaningful interaction.

7.4 Adapting Communication Styles: Tailoring Your Approach

EXECUTIVEness requires adaptable communication that resonates with diverse audiences and situations, adjusting the approach to suit different individuals and contexts.

Think of it as crafting a customized set of words and tones for each interaction. Whether you're addressing a team meeting or having a one-on-one conversation, the key is understanding the nuances that make each audience unique.

Recognize that communication preferences vary widely. Some team members thrive on data and facts, while others resonate with stories that tap into their emotions. By embracing this diversity, you create an environment where everyone feels valued and heard.

> MASTERING THE ART OF ADAPTING COMMUNICATION STYLES INVOLVES KEEN OBSERVATION, EMPATHY, AND FLEXIBILITY. IT'S ABOUT PAYING ATTENTION TO HOW YOUR MESSAGE IS RECEIVED AND ADJUSTING YOUR APPROACH TO ENHANCE UNDERSTANDING.

This practice not only fosters better engagement but also highlights your commitment to practice EXECUTIVEness at every level.

7.5 Nonverbal Communication: The Silent Language of Superior Leadership

Imagine a symphony where the conductor doesn't utter a word but conveys emotions and directions through graceful gestures. In leadership, nonverbal communication is your conductor's baton, guiding the orchestra of interaction with subtlety and nuance.

Your posture, eye contact, gestures, and even your aura communicate more profoundly than words alone. The firm handshake that exudes confidence, the nod of affirmation that shows attentiveness, the genuine smile that welcomes collaboration – these are the notes that compose the symphony of leadership.

Harnessing the power of nonverbal communication is about aligning your words with your body language. When your actions and expressions harmonize, they create an authentic and resonant message. Maintaining eye contact during conversations demonstrates respect and engagement, while an open posture fosters approachability.

Just as a conductor's baton communicates the tempo and mood of a piece, your nonverbal cues set the tone for interactions. They infuse your words with sincerity, empathy, and credibility, making your communication not just audible but truly impactful.

These elements, the adaptation of communication styles and the orchestration of nonverbal cues, converge to amplify your impact and presence, painting a portrait that resonates in every interaction.

MASTERING THE SILENT LANGUAGE OF NONVERBAL
COMMUNICATION IS A VITAL SKILL. IT CROSSES
CULTURAL DIVIDES, AMPLIFIES YOUR AUTHENTICITY,
AND ENSURES YOUR LEADERSHIP RESONATES DEEPLY
WITH EVERYONE WHO EXPERIENCES IT.

7.6 Feedback that Fuels Growth: Constructive Communication

In the journey towards *EXECUTIVEness*, feedback is the compass that guides individuals toward growth and excellence. It's not merely a commentary on past actions; it's a pathway to continuous improvement. Yet, delivering feedback is a fine art that requires skill, understanding, and strategic intention.

Imagine a sculptor who delicately chisels away at a block of marble to reveal a masterpiece. Similarly, constructive feedback is about chiseling away at behaviors or actions that hinder progress, allowing the talent within each individual to shine through. It's not a blunt instrument; it's a precision tool that, when wielded adeptly, shapes growth and development.

Although most understand that feedback should never feel like an attack, but a channel to encourage improvement, sometimes emotion takes over and its purpose gets lost in translation.

To avoid being delivered or received as a negative non-constructive comment or reprimand, constructive feedback must be specific, actionable, and forward-focused. It doesn't only have to highlight shortcomings; but offer insights and solutions that empower individuals to evolve.

Remember, your feedback is a compass that not only points out directions for improvement but also illuminates the strengths that can propel individuals forward.

> WHEN FEEDBACK IS DELIVERED WITH EMPATHY AND RESPECT, IT FOSTERS TRUST, CONFIDENCE, AND A SHARED COMMITMENT TO GROWTH.

7.7 Influence through Storytelling: Weaving Narratives for Impact

Visualize a boardroom where a leader stands before a team, armed with data-filled slides projected onto a screen. The numbers tell a story of increased quarterly sales, higher customer satisfaction, and improved operational efficiency. These metrics are impressive, but they remain cold and detached, lacking the power to truly resonate.

Now, consider an alternative scenario. The same leader steps forward, but this time, instead of diving straight into the data, they pause and take a deep breath. With a genuine smile, they share a story. It's a story of Sarah, a resolute customer satisfaction representative who addressed an escalation. As the leader speaks, a graph appears on the screen, illustrating the number of hours Sarah invested.

But this isn't just any graph – it's a visual narrative. The graph's peaks and valleys coincide with Sarah's journey, highlighting her moments of dedication and persistence. The numbers, while important, now serve as landmarks in a human story of determination and impact. As the leader continues, they reveal how Sarah's unwavering commitment led to increased customer satisfaction scores, exemplified by another graph that shows a steep upward trend.

Here, the leader isn't merely presenting data; they're conveying a message that transcends numbers. They're painting a picture of Sarah's dedication, resilience, and the difference she made. The team isn't just processing statistics; they're connecting with the humanity behind the metrics. The impact is palpable, and the lesson is clear: Behind every data point, there's a story waiting to be told.

Since the dawn of humanity, stories have been the heartbeat of human connection. From ancient myths to modern novels, stories captivate our imagination and awaken our emotions. In leadership, storytelling is a tool that can elevate your messages from ordinary to extraordinary.

Storytelling in leadership is about infusing your messages with the human touch that transforms information into inspiration.

A graph may display trends, but a well-told story takes those trends and adds context, emotion, and relatability. It invites your team to see themselves in the narrative and encourages them to contribute to the story's evolution.

As you master the art of weaving narratives into your leadership communication, consider how you can leverage visual aids like graphs, charts, and infographics to enhance the storytelling experience.

> BY PAIRING DATA WITH A HUMAN-CENTERED NARRATIVE, YOU CAN CREATE POWERFUL MESSAGES THAT LEAVE A LASTING IMPACT AND INFLUENCE PEOPLE'S PERSPECTIVES, MOTIVATIONS AND ACTIONS.

7.8 Navigating Difficult Conversations: Courageous Communication

EXECUTIVEness isn't always a stroll on a well-paved path; sometimes, it's a journey through challenging terrain. Difficult conversations, like uncharted territories, demand courageous communication – a blend of empathy, tact, and assertiveness that navigates sensitive topics while preserving the foundation of trust.

Imagine a tightrope walker poised high above, balancing carefully with each step. Navigating difficult conversations requires a similar balance between asserting your message and respecting the emotions of others. It's about acknowledging discomfort while fostering an atmosphere where open dialogue can flourish.

Difficult conversations can arise from conflicts, performance issues, or even organizational changes. Courageous communication is about addressing these topics head-on, without avoidance or delay. It involves active listening to understand perspectives, empathy to acknowledge emotions, and assertiveness to convey your message clearly.

Avoiding difficult conversations is a disservice to all. By engaging in these conversations with grace and courage, you show that you value growth, respect, and collaboration. You create a culture where challenges are opportunities for growth and where conflicts are steppingstones toward resolution.

THE PATH OF COURAGEOUS COMMUNICATION IS NOT ABOUT WINNING DEBATES; IT'S ABOUT FOSTERING UNDERSTANDING AND FINDING SOLUTIONS. IT'S A TESTAMENT TO YOUR COMMITMENT TO YOUR TEAM'S WELL-BEING AND PROGRESS.

As you face challenging conversations, you'll uncover the resilience that thrives in honest dialogue, and you'll lay the groundwork for stronger relationships and lasting trust.

7.9 Communicating Change: Leading Through Transitions

Change – a constant force that shapes organizations, challenges individuals, and demands adept communication.

Navigating change isn't about announcing plans; it's about orchestrating a communication strategy that reassures, aligns, and empowers. Change communication isn't a monologue; it's a dialogue that acknowledges individual experiences, encourages collaboration, and ensures that the entire organization moves forward as a unified force.

Picture your organization on the brink of transformation, ready to implement a meaningful change initiative. As a Superior Leader, you must step forward, aware that conveying change requires more than directives; it demands a narrative that navigates uncertainty with clarity and compassion.

To this purpose, I recommend adopting a process that I call *The Simplified Three-step Approach: Inform, Empathize, and Guide.*

- **Step 1- Inform:** Initiate the communication by clearly outlining the rationale, goals, and potential impact of the change.

- **Step 2- Empathize:** Then, pivot to empathy, acknowledging the apprehensions and concerns of the team. Sharing personal anecdotes of navigating change, bridge the gap between the organizational decision and its human implications.

- **Step 3- Guide:** Finally, guide the team towards the future, outlining the roadmap and emphasizing their role in this change journey.

> BY PAINTING A VIVID PICTURE OF THE DESTINATION, YOU INSPIRE CONFIDENCE AND ENGAGEMENT, TRANSFORMING CHANGE FROM A DAUNTING DISRUPTION INTO A COLLECTIVE ENDEAVOR FUELED BY PURPOSE.

However, effective change communication also involves actively listening to feedback and creating an environment where team members feel heard and valued. Establishing open channels for feedback ensures that concerns can be addressed promptly and transparently. Continuous support and updates throughout the change process maintain momentum and trust.

Understanding the true form of empathy at work and the importance of applying it is crucial. Empathy isn't just a guiding force but a bridge to successful leadership.

When you communicate change the right way, you create a culture of resilience and adaptability. You empower your team to embrace change with a sense of ownership and optimism, knowing they are part of a larger purpose and that their contributions matter.

7.10 Authentic Leadership Communication: Aligning Words and Actions

As an authentic leader, your actions speak as loudly as your words. When you communicate, your team doesn't just listen to the message—they connect with the values and intentions behind it.

In your leadership role, you actively participate in the work alongside your team, demonstrating that leadership isn't just about delegation. For example, if your team is working late to meet a deadline, you stay with them, showing solidarity and commitment. This direct approach builds trust and shows that you're in the trenches with them.

You foster innovation by creating an environment where ideas can flourish, rather than just talking about it. This means setting up regular brainstorming sessions, encouraging out-of-the-box thinking, and providing resources for experimental projects. When a team member suggests an original approach, you not only listen but also discuss the feasibility and potential impact, showing genuine interest and support.

Authentic leadership communication transcends scripted speeches. It involves expressing genuine thoughts, concerns, and aspirations. For instance, during a team meeting, you might share your own challenges and how you overcame them, making your leadership more relatable. Admitting mistakes is also crucial; if a project doesn't go as planned, openly acknowledging your part in it and discussing lessons learned fosters a culture of accountability and continuous improvement.

Seeking feedback is another vital aspect. Ask your team for their insights and opinions on both projects and your leadership. This can be done through anonymous surveys or open forums, ensuring everyone feels safe to speak up. By incorporating their feedback, you show that you value their input and are committed to growing alongside them.

By embracing authentic communication, you foster an environment where open dialogue thrives, inspiring a deeper sense of ownership and commitment among your team members. When your words and actions align, you not only lead but also inspire your team to embody the same authenticity in their roles.

7.11 Executive Presence through Communication: Radiating *EXECUTIVEness*

Imagine yourself entering a room, your presence commanding attention even before you speak. Visualize a scenario where you step on a stage to address a large audience. Your posture exudes confidence, and your tone carries authority.

Is this scenario you don't merely convey information; you radiate leadership through your communication style. Every gesture, intonation, and expression exudes authenticity. You acknowledge each question with respect, even if you

don't have immediate answers. By embodying humility and assertiveness, you foster an environment where collaboration flourishes.

This is *EXECUTIVEness* at its best, this is executive presence – a quality that elevates leadership communication beyond words. When you radiate executive presence through communication, you set a standard of professionalism and inspire others to excel.

> EXECUTIVE PRESENCE ISN'T ABOUT ADOPTING A FACADE; IT'S ABOUT INTERNALIZING LEADERSHIP VALUES AND PROJECTING THEM OUTWARD. IT'S ABOUT BEING FULLY PRESENT IN EACH INTERACTION, WHETHER IT'S A ONE-ON-ONE CONVERSATION OR A HIGH-STAKES PRESENTATION.

7.12 Translating It All into Action: Elevating Your Communication

To truly embody *EXECUTIVEness*, it's imperative to bridge theory with practice. Communication skills are honed through action, not mere reflection. Here, I present you with four exercises that consolidate your understanding and empower you to elevate your communication prowess.

Exercise: Communication Audit

Take a moment to assess recent communication interactions. Were you attentive and empathetic during conversations? Did you adapt your style to diverse audiences? Reflect on instances where your communication aligned with the principles we discussed and areas where improvement is possible. This audit helps you identify strengths and opportunities for growth.

Exercise: Purposeful Storytelling

Craft a short story that encapsulates a leadership lesson or experience. Consider the narrative's authenticity, relevance, and emotional resonance. Share this story with a trusted colleague or mentor and gather feedback. This exercise hones your storytelling skills and demonstrates how purposeful narratives forge connections that resonate with others.

Exercise: Nonverbal Communication Challenge

Record a brief video of yourself communicating a message. Observe your body language, facial expressions, and gestures. Analyze how these nonverbal cues enhance or detract from your message's impact. This exercise heightens your awareness of nonverbal cues, enabling you to fine-tune your delivery.

Exercise: Courageous Conversation Simulation

Envision a challenging conversation you may encounter as a leader – delivering tough feedback, addressing conflict, or navigating ambiguity. Script your approach, keeping in mind the principles of empathy and assertiveness. Role-play the scenario with a colleague, alternating roles. This exercise enhances your ability to approach difficult conversations with confidence and sensitivity.

Incorporating these exercises into your leadership journey nurtures your communication skills, allowing you to consistently communicate with purpose, impact and influence.

> COMMUNICATION IS A DYNAMIC ART THAT EVOLVES WITH PRACTICE. BY EMBRACING THESE EXERCISES, YOU TRANSCEND THEORY, CHANNELING THE ESSENCE OF THIS CHAPTER INTO TANGIBLE OUTCOMES.

Chapter 8:

Inspiring Teams: A Journey of Empowerment

Now, let's explore the art of inspiring teams, focusing on creating a culture of excellence within your team. At the heart of this chapter lies the essence of leadership inspiration.

8.1 The Essence of Team Inspiration: Cultivating a Vision of Excellence

In the dynamic landscape of leadership, the ability to inspire teams is a hallmark of extraordinary leaders. Chapter 8 explores how *EXECUTIVEness* instills inspiration within teams, ignites their passion, and propels them toward greatness. This journey offers a blueprint for creating a culture of excellence that resonates with every team member.

The Power of Leadership Inspiration

At the core of team inspiration lies the transformative power of leadership. When you radiate enthusiasm, commitment, and a compelling vision, you have the unique ability to rally your team around shared goals. Through your actions and words, you can craft a narrative that transcends the ordinary and sparks a collective sense of purpose.

> LEADERSHIP INSPIRATION IS NOT DRIVEN BY MERE
> CHARISMA, BUT BY A DEEP UNDERSTANDING OF A
> MULTI-LAYERED APPROACH THAT INCORPORATES
> COMMUNICATION, EMPATHY, AND AUTHENTICITY.

EXECUTIVEness as a Catalyst

EXECUTIVEness goes beyond individual competence; it extends to team dynamics. When you embody these principles, you are able to align your team's aspirations with the organization's mission. You then are capable to communicate clearly, setting forth a vision that resonates with team members' values and aspirations. In doing so, you lay the foundation for a culture that strives for excellence, embraces challenges, and supports one another in their pursuit of collective success.

The Ripple Effect of Excellence

As team members witness your dedication to clear communication, empathetic understanding, and genuine connection, they are naturally motivated to mirror these qualities. The culture of excellence permeates through the team, encouraging collaboration, innovation, and a shared commitment to achieving remarkable outcomes. You become the catalyst for a positive transformation, propelling the team toward success and creating an environment where each member contributes their best efforts, collectively achieving extraordinary results.

The Blueprint Ahead

In the upcoming sections of this chapter, we'll go deeper into the nuances of team inspiration. We'll explore practical strategies for igniting enthusiasm, fostering collaboration, and cultivating a sense of ownership among team members. From fostering open dialogue to recognizing individual contributions, this approach forms the backbone of each strategy, breathing life into your leadership journey.

Keep in mind that inspiring teams isn't a mere task – it's a continuous journey of growth and refinement. Through this lens, we will discuss vital approaches that will help you foster an environment where every team member is empowered to reach their full potential, contributing to a collective vision of excellence.

8.2 Empowerment through Clear Direction: Aligning Goals and Values

In leadership, alignment isn't a mere buzzword – it's a strategic lever that transforms teams from functioning entities into thriving powerhouses.

The path to empowerment often commences with clarity and alignment, and that's precisely where Ed's story becomes known.

Value Driving Results:

Last summer, I was approached by Ed, a seasoned sales leader who was grappling with a very particular problem. The company had an excellent product, a fantastic marketing strategy with a well-defined audience, and an extensive customer base. Sales teams were surpassing all goals without negatively impacting financials, production, or product quality. However, there was a particular area that showed a continuous decline – customer loyalty.

Noticing this trend, Ed implemented new client services processes for established customers, with a robust customer-centric post-sale process. But despite his efforts, something was amiss. Ed reached out to us, seeking solutions beyond his own perspective.

During our sessions, the true nature of the challenge became clear: alignment.

The root cause of declining customer satisfaction wasn't confined to the post-sales process; it was a result of the sales approach itself. Ed's teams were heavily compensated for conversion, and in the process, they had lost sight of the customer and the product's intrinsic value.

Guided by these newfound principles, we set aside the conventional approach and embraced audacity and resourcefulness. Our methodology was as daring as it was innovative, one that would shed light on the underlying weakness for the entire organization to see. This plan aimed to tackle the issue head-on, taking a trailblazing route that reached and engaged departments that might have seemed disconnected from the problem at hand. The directive was clear: a comprehensive realignment of the sales process with the very core values that defined his company.

Ed's journey commenced with fostering collaborative sessions between the sales team, product developers, financial experts, and key executives. The focus was to reignite their connection to the company's mission, vision, values and products. This dynamic exchange of ideas not only revived their appreciation for the value they brought to the client, but also instilled a profound customer-centric ethos.

But Ed's transformational journey didn't halt at realignment. Recognizing that empowerment hinges on ownership, he revamped the compensation structure. New incentives and bonuses tied directly to customer satisfaction metrics injected vigor into the team's pursuit of excellence.

The result? A brief dip followed by an exponential ascent. Ed's sales and customer services teams set unprecedented records.

Ed's story underscores the profound impact of aligning goals and values. It's a testament to how a sharp vision of values serves as the North Star, guiding teams toward empowered action and unparalleled success.

8.3 Adopting a Sense of Empowerment: Encouraging Ownership and Autonomy

When considering leadership, there's usually one aspect that often gets overlooked—the power of empowerment. Leaders usually focus on strategy, vision, and decision-making, but the true strength of a leader lies in their ability to empower their team. This notion extends beyond the boundaries of theory and finds its roots in daily practice.

Empowerment in Practice

Empowerment is more than a leadership buzzword; it is the practical application of trust, autonomy, and responsibility within a team. When leaders empower their team members, they are saying, "I trust you to make decisions, take initiative, and contribute to our shared goals." This trust fosters a sense of ownership and accountability that cannot be achieved through top-down directives alone.

Creating an Empowered Environment

To cultivate empowerment, leaders must:

1. **Delegate Responsibility**: Entrust team members with meaningful tasks and decision-making power. This not only

builds their confidence but also demonstrates your trust in their abilities.

2. **Encourage Innovation**: Create a safe space for creativity and experimentation. Allow your team to propose and evaluate innovative ideas without fear of failure.

3. **Provide Resources and Support**: Ensure your team has the necessary tools, training, and support to succeed. Empowerment is not about leaving people to fend for themselves; it is about enabling them to thrive.

4. **Recognize and Reward Contributions**: Acknowledge the efforts and achievements of your team members. Recognition reinforces their value to the team and encourages continued excellence.

The Ripple Effect of Empowerment

When empowerment is practiced consistently, it creates a ripple effect throughout the organization. Empowered team members are more likely to:

- **Take Initiative**: They proactively seek solutions and opportunities for improvement.

- **Collaborate Effectively**: They work together towards common goals, leveraging each other's strengths.

- **Demonstrate Loyalty**: They feel valued and respected, which fosters an intense sense of loyalty and commitment to the organization.

Empowerment as a Continuous Practice

Empowerment is not a one-time effort; it is a continuous practice that requires regular reflection and adjustment. Leaders must remain attuned to their team's needs and be willing to adapt their approach as circumstances change. By making empowerment a fundamental part of their leadership style, leaders can unlock the full potential of their teams and drive sustained success.

In summary, the power of empowerment in leadership is profound. It goes beyond theoretical discussions and manifests in the everyday actions and decisions of a leader. By empowering their teams, leaders not only enhance individual performance but also build a culture of trust, innovation, and collective achievement.

Allow me to share another practical example, this one underscoring the transformative impact of empowerment.

Ownership and Autonomy when nothing else works!

I had the privilege of mentoring Nadia, a rising leader grappling with the challenges of a new leadership role.

One of her tasks was orchestrating a team schedule that not only aligned with business needs but also catered to the individual preferences of her 12-member team. Nadia's attempts yielded versions that satisfied no one entirely. The tussle between personal needs and operational requirements created conflicts and discontent.

That's when I suggested a simple but radical idea for her—let the team craft the schedule themselves. Although skeptical, Nadia embraced the concept and called for an all-hands meeting. For two hours, the team engaged in a vigorous discussion (without Nadia's presence) that culminated in a compromise. No one was ecstatic about the outcome, yet everyone acknowledged the necessity of mutual concessions.

This story isn't about reaching a schedule consensus; it addresses the importance of the dynamics of empowerment, ownership, and autonomy. By entrusting her team with the responsibility of resolving a challenge, Nadia displayed her faith in their abilities and helped them understand the complexity of decision-making and compromise.

The lesson here reverberates—the act of empowering your team is a recognition of their capabilities, an acknowledgment of their expertise, and an invitation to embrace challenges and fostering a culture that values compromise in navigating complex decisions.

> RAISING A SENSE OF BELONGING AND COHESIVENESS WITHIN A TEAM STEMS FROM GRANTING THEM THE AUTONOMY TO CHART THEIR COURSE, TO TAKE OWNERSHIP OF THEIR ACTIONS, AND TO THRIVE AS A COLLECTIVE FORCE.

8.4 Transparent and Open Dialogue: The Crucial Role of Communication in Inspiration

EXECUTIVEness doesn't just manifest in decisions made or goals achieved; it thrives in the quality of communication nurtured within a team, where transparent and open dialogue reigns supreme.

Communication isn't just a means to convey information; it's the lifeline of inspiration. When harnessed effectively, communication serves as the conduit through which ideas flow, concerns are addressed, and visions are shared. In fostering inspiration, communication bridges aspirations and realization. By leveraging EXECUTIVEness principles, you can cultivate transparent communication. This involves creating an environment where individuals feel empowered to express their thoughts, voice their concerns, and contribute to collective growth.

The power of transparent communication lies in its ability to instill trust, eliminate assumptions, and discover the path forward with clarity.

Let's illustrate this with an example: imagine a team faced with a complex project deadline. Through open dialogue, team members share diverse perspectives on how to approach the task, ensuring all angles are considered and decisions are well-informed.

But transparency alone is not enough. Open dialogue—an active exchange of ideas and perspectives—is the driving force that propels teams toward innovation. It's within this space that the sparks of creativity ignite, and diverse viewpoints converge to mold breakthrough concepts.

> WHEN TEAMS ENGAGE IN CANDID CONVERSATIONS WITHOUT FEAR OF JUDGMENT OR REPRISAL, CONSTRUCTIVE COLLABORATION, CREATIVITY AND OWNERSHIP FLOURISHES.

Let's explore strategies for creating safe spaces that encourage dialogue, crafting messages that inspire action, and weaving authenticity into every word spoken.

Creating Safe Spaces for Open Dialogue

People thrive in environments where open dialogue is nurtured. Embracing openness means fostering an atmosphere where team members feel safe to express their opinions, ideas, and concerns.

You can achieve this by establishing regular feedback sessions, town hall meetings, or informal coffee chats—opportunities for team members to voice their thoughts without fear of judgment.

Transparent communication allows for the exchange of diverse perspectives, which can lead to innovative solutions. When team members sense that their opinions are valued and their voices are heard, a culture of collaboration and belonging emerges.

Weaving Authenticity into Every Word

Authenticity is the solid foundation for building trust and rapport. Early on, I discovered the pitfalls of pedestals; they're traps, mere invitations to inevitable falls. Instead, I encourage leaders to share their experiences, successes, and failures openly. This vulnerability humanizes leadership, fostering a culture of confidence and respect among team members.

Admitting uncertainties and seeking input not only builds trust but also promotes collaborative problem-solving. This approach, grounded in authenticity, empowers both you and your team to navigate challenges with resilience and inspiration.

Your ability to embrace this approach will undoubtedly elevate your *EXECUTIVEness* and empower those around you.

> BY NURTURING OPEN DIALOGUE, CRAFTING INSPIRING MESSAGES, AND WEAVING AUTHENTICITY INTO YOUR DIALOGUE, YOU'RE CULTIVATING AN ENVIRONMENT WHERE INSPIRATION FLOURISHES AND LEADERSHIP THRIVES.

8.5 Translating It All into Action: Motivating and Empowering Teams through the Application of *EXECUTIVEness*

As we draw this chapter to a close, it's time to transition from theory to practice. The principles of *EXECUTIVEness* that we've explored throughout this chapter are not meant to remain abstract concepts; they are tools to be wielded in leadership. Now is the moment to embark on the journey of application—to roll up your sleeves and integrate these strategies into your leadership approach.

Reflect:

Begin by reflecting on your current practices. How aligned are they with the principles of empowerment, clear direction, open communication, and fostering a sense of belonging?

Identify:

Identify areas where you can introduce changes and improvements. You could initiate team discussions that allow everyone to contribute their ideas freely or experiment with crafting messages that resonate on a deeper level.

Observe:

Observe how your team responds to your efforts and make adjustments accordingly. Acknowledge that mistakes might happen along the way, but these too provide invaluable learning opportunities.

Remember that transformation doesn't happen overnight. It's a gradual process of evolution and refinement. Implement one strategy at a time and assess its impact.

As you put these concepts into action, keep your finger on the pulse of your team's progress. Is the atmosphere becoming more inclusive? Are your messages igniting enthusiasm and action? Are team members taking ownership and embracing autonomy? Regularly seek feedback from your team and be willing to adapt your approach based on their insights.

> ***EXECUTIVENESS*** IS A COLLABORATIVE ENDEAVOR. ENGAGE WITH YOUR TEAM, LEARN FROM YOUR PEERS, AND CONTINUE TO REFINE YOUR APPROACH. THE JOURNEY IS DYNAMIC AND EVER EVOLVING, AND YOUR COMMITMENT TO CONNECT WILL UNDOUBTEDLY GUIDE YOU TOWARD UNPARALLELED LEADERSHIP SUCCESS.

Chapter 9:

Infusing *EXECUTIVEness* in your Daily Practice – Practical Steps to Seamlessly Apply Skills

Now's the moment to initiate the transformative process of embedding *EXECUTIVEness* principles into your daily leadership routine. As you've discovered throughout this book, this process requires a fusion of intellect, emotional acumen, and the audacity to question conventions.

By incorporating these principles into your daily routine, you're elevating your leadership effectiveness and sowing the seeds of a culture of excellence within your team and organization.

View leadership through a dynamic lens, adopting the habit of probing, inquiring, and discerning. It encourages you to challenge the status quo, disrupt familiar patterns, see things through a multifaceted perspective.

As you practice these principles daily, you'll cultivate the skill of thinking beyond the ordinary, the art of unearthing innovative solutions that lie beyond the surface. You'll learn to balance audacity with measured judgment, to step out of your comfort zone while weighing the risks.

Through this integration, you'll find yourself navigating uncharted waters, redefining limits, and generating outcomes that stand out.

> BY INCORPORATING **EXECUTIVENESS** INTO YOUR DAILY LEADERSHIP ROUTINE, YOU'RE NOT JUST ALTERING YOUR ACTIONS—YOU'RE SHAPING YOUR LEADERSHIP MENTAL PATTERN. THIS PATTERN GUIDES YOUR APPROACH, DECISIONS, AND INTERACTIONS. IT ENABLES YOU TO LEAD WITH UNWAVERING AUTHENTICITY, RESILIENCE, AND THE UNRELENTING PURSUIT OF EXCELLENCE.

So, why is it crucial to adopt and practice these principles daily? By fostering a mindset of inquiry, analysis, and innovation, you're pioneering a leadership style that goes beyond the conventional and paves the way for transformative change.

9.1 The Power of Consistency: The habit making process.

I can still recall the cringe-worthy sounds of my daughter Bella's early violin days in elementary school. What began as screeching gradually evolved into a decent tune, thanks to her daily practice—prompted by me, though I wasn't always thrilled about it. This was the beginning of her journey to becoming first chair in high school.

It's a simple yet profound lesson in the unexpected rewards of consistency. Whether it's your first concert, a tennis victory, a successful holiday dinner, or an outstanding presentation, these moments highlight the power of sticking to your efforts.

Consistency forms the bedrock of success in any endeavor, including leadership. By consistently questioning, innovating, and daring to venture into new territories, you're not just doing things; you're embodying a transformative perspective on life.

Creating habits is a journey that can take two distinct paths: one where you genuinely love what you do, and the other where you intentionally invest effort to develop that love. As you apply these principles, I encourage you to follow the former.

Approach them with an open mind and a willingness to appreciate the profound transformation they can bring to your leadership approach. It's the art of falling in love with the process that holds the key to lasting change. By consistently integrating these principles, you'll find them becoming intertwined with your leadership style organically.

Just as you develop an appreciation for a new skill through dedicated practice, these principles will weave into the fabric of your daily routines. Over time, what once required conscious effort will become instinctual—a habit rooted in genuine engagement. Embracing these principles will shape your interactions, decisions, and the overall culture of your team.

Better Late than Never?

Consider the case of one of my mentees who struggled with punctuality. She loved being productive and often worked until the last minute, leading to frequent tardiness for meetings. This habit left no room for unforeseen delays like unexpected conversations or elevator stops. She disliked waiting idly or engaging in small talk before meetings, making it challenging to adjust her routine.

To address this, we agreed that a deliberate process was the best option to change her behavior.

Here are the illustrative steps:

Identify the Goal: Recognize that a change is needed and set a specific goal, such as arriving five minutes early for meetings.

Understand Motivation: Find intrinsic motivation by focusing on the benefits, such as reducing stress and showing respect for others' time.

Break it Down: Divide the goal into manageable steps. For instance, leave the desk 10 minutes before the meeting starts.

Create a Routine: Establish a pre-meeting routine that includes wrapping up tasks early and mentally preparing for the meeting.

Adjust Mindset: Embrace the waiting time as an opportunity to collect thoughts or connect with colleagues.

Track Progress: Monitor adherence to the new routine and celebrate milestones, like consistently arriving early.

Persist and Adapt: Overcome setbacks by staying committed and adjusting strategies as needed.

Creating habits can be transformative, whether it's arriving on time for meetings or mastering a new skill. This example illustrates the power of persistence and strategy in habit formation. By identifying specific goals, understanding motivations, and breaking down tasks into manageable steps, you can effectively cultivate new behaviors.

Embrace each challenge as an opportunity for growth and celebrate every milestone along the way. Remember, habits are not just actions; they shape your identity and influence your leadership journey. As you integrate these principles into your daily life, you're not just practicing habits—you're embodying a new way of being that enhances your leadership effectiveness and inspires those around you.

9.2 Self-Reflection for Growth: Learning from Leadership Experiences

I didn't invite you to a quest for perfection but to a journey to the top. It means acknowledging the human element, where errors and missteps are part of the process. This 'Boldness' comes from understanding that every venture might not yield the intended outcome, and that's perfectly alright. It's the courage to move forward regardless, to 'Do,' knowing that experiencing setbacks isn't a sign of failure but a signal that you're in the game.

However, it's essential to regularly set aside time to review your recent interactions, decisions, and their outcomes. Ask yourself candidly: What went well? What could have been managed differently? With this mindset, self-reflection becomes your compass for improvement.

Practical Steps for Self-Reflection:

- **Schedule Regular Reflection Time:** Set aside dedicated periods weekly or monthly to review recent experiences and decisions.

- **Use a Journal or Notes:** Keep a journal or use digital notes to jot down reflections and insights.

- **Ask Critical Questions:** Challenge yourself with specific questions like "What did I learn from this situation?" or "How could I have approached this differently?"

- **Seek Feedback:** Actively seek feedback from peers, mentors, or team members to gain different perspectives.

In these moments, you're embracing 'Openness' to acknowledge areas that need growth. It's about humbly accepting your limitations and using self-reflection as a 'Guiding' tool to navigate the path forward.

Practical Steps for Openness:

- **Accept Feedback Gracefully:** Be open to constructive criticism and view it as an opportunity to improve.

- **Practice Active Listening:** Listen attentively to others' viewpoints without defensiveness.

- **Encourage Dialogue:** Foster an environment where team members feel comfortable sharing ideas and concerns openly.

From acceptance and self-reflection springs the 'Adaptability' phase. This is where you apply the lessons learned to refine your approach.

Practical Steps for Adaptability:

- **Iterate Based on Feedback:** Adjust your strategies based on insights gained from self-reflection and feedback.

- **Stay Agile:** Be ready to pivot and change course when circumstances require it.

- **Encourage Experimentation:** Allow yourself and your team to experiment with novel approaches.

Finally, through this journey, you discover 'Growth'—the ultimate ingredient of *EXECUTIVEness* that stems from your willingness to embrace the process, learn, and evolve. Your team watches as you walk this path, and it sets an inspiring example. They see the strength in acknowledging imperfections, in self-reflecting, in adapting, and in pursuing growth.

Practical Steps for Growth:

- **Set Development Goals:** Continually set goals that challenge you to grow professionally and personally.

- **Celebrate Progress:** Acknowledge milestones and improvements made through your journey of growth.

- **Encourage Continuous Learning:** Foster a culture of learning within your team by sharing insights and encouraging skill development.

> THE PATH TO SUCCESS IS PAVED BY BOLDNESS, OPENNESS, MISTAKES AND ULTIMATELY ADAPTATION. IT'S A JOURNEY THAT SHAPES LEADERS WHO AREN'T AFRAID TO MAKE ERR, TO LEARN, AND TO TRANSFORM THEMSELVES FOR THE BETTER.

9.3 Building a Supportive Leadership Network: Collaborative Leadership

The journey for constant growth is far from solitary. Rather, it's a collaborative expedition that thrives in the company of others who share your drive for growth and excellence.

Let me share a story from my experience as a Marketing Compliance Leader, which vividly illustrates the remarkable outcomes of collaborative leadership.

Collaboration at its best!

In my role, ensuring the quality of guest interactions was paramount, specially interactions via telephone. To that end, we searched for advanced tools to monitor these interaction, and my team devised a plan to acquire voice analytics technology.

Once the proposal got the green light, we ventured beyond our immediate sphere and engaged with an unexpected ally—the Collections Department. Surprisingly, their operations closely mirrored ours in unexpected ways, revealing a shared challenge: optimizing call center operations and quality control.

With collaborative leadership at the forefront, we combined resources, ideas, and expertise. The result? A seamless partnership that defied conventional boundaries.

Together, we drastically cut costs, streamlined resource allocations, and shared invaluable insights. Our once-isolated teams transformed into synchronized symphony, leveraging shared goals and mutual support for optimal efficiency.

Why Collaborative Leadership Matters

This tale isn't unique; it's a testament to the strength of collaboration. Seeking partnerships beyond your usual scope enriches your perspective, fuels innovation, and fosters a sense of shared accomplishment. Through this lens, leadership isn't confined—it's an expansive network that thrives on collective wisdom and shared achievement.

Practical Steps for Fostering Collaborative Leadership:

Identify Common Goals: Look for areas where your objectives overlap with other departments or teams.

Initiate Open Dialogue: Foster communication channels that encourage sharing ideas and challenges.

Build Trust: Invest time in building relationships and trust with potential collaborators.

Celebrate Successes: Recognize and celebrate achievements that result from collaborative efforts.

> BUILDING A SUPPORTIVE LEADERSHIP NETWORK THROUGH COLLABORATION ISN'T JUST ABOUT EFFICIENCY—IT'S ABOUT CREATING A CULTURE OF INNOVATION AND MUTUAL SUPPORT THAT TRANSCENDS ORGANIZATIONAL BOUNDARIES. EMBRACE COLLABORATION AS A STRATEGIC TOOL TO AMPLIFY YOUR IMPACT AND DRIVE COLLECTIVE SUCCESS.

9.4 Translating It All into Action: A Holistic Approach to Daily Leadership

As you've journeyed through this chapter, you've gained profound insights into how you can revolutionize your leadership style. Now, let's translate these insights into tangible action steps. Here's how to take this concept from theory to transformative practice:

Craft Your Personalized Action Plan:

Begin by crafting an action plan that encapsulates the principles discussed throughout this book. Set specific, achievable goals for each day, week, and month. For example, commit to dedicating the first 15 minutes of your day to intentional reflection, assessing your actions and decisions against the principles you've learned.

Schedule Reflective Moments:

Designate regular moments of reflection, not just at the end of the day, but throughout it. Pause for five minutes after meetings or significant interactions. Ask yourself: What could have been done differently? Reflective moments foster a habit of continuous learning.

Cultivate Collaborative Habits:

Actively nurture relationships with fellow leaders who share your commitment to succeed with heart, brain, and soul. Schedule regular meetups or virtual calls to discuss challenges, share insights, and seek fresh perspectives. Collaborative habits amplify your collective wisdom and elevate your leadership game.

Embrace a Holistic Approach:

Take into account all facets of your leadership. From team meetings to one-on-one discussions, weave in elements of boldness, authenticity, and the drive for excellence. By doing so, you're embedding these principles into the very DNA of your leadership style.

Revise and Refine:

Just as leadership evolves, your approach should too. Regularly revisit and refine your action plan. Adapt it to your changing circumstances and evolving insights. Remain flexible and open to growth, ensuring your leadership journey remains dynamic and responsive.

By committing to these actionable steps, you're not only embracing transformative leadership practices but also setting a course for continual growth and impact. Let these principles guide your daily actions, shaping a leadership style that inspires and achieves remarkable results.

THROUGH CONSISTENCY, SELF-REFLECTION, COLLABORATION, AND A COMPREHENSIVE APPROACH, YOU'RE PROPELLING YOURSELF TOWARD IMPACTFUL LEADERSHIP THAT'S ROOTED IN AUTHENTICITY AND CONTINUOUS IMPROVEMENT.

Chapter 10:

Leading with Clarity and Impact: Concluding Insights on Exemplary Approach Guided by *EXECUTIVEness*

It's time to pivot our focus to two essential pillars: achieving unmistakable clarity and leaving a meaningful impact. While our journey may have ventured into sometimes theorical waters, practical application demands a resolute and straightforward approach. Ahead, we will explore how to infuse every aspect of leadership with clarity and intent.

Leadership, fundamentally, requires clear and well-defined strategies, decisions, and communications. There is no room for uncertainty, vagueness, or ambiguity. *EXECUTIVEness* thrives on our ability to provide clear direction and create palpable impact.

10.1 Clarity: The Foundation of *EXECUTIVEness*

Within the core of *EXECUTIVEness* lies a vital cornerstone — clarity. This chapter will delve into the essence of clarity's role, stripping away complexities to reveal the power of straightforward intent.

Allow me to illustrate the significance of clarity with a childhood memory.

When I was 5 years old, our apartment building was relatively close to a zoo. My mom would take my brother and me to the terrace to gaze at animals. "Look at the elephants," my mom would say, pointing into the distance. "Where, where?" I'd inquire, squinting. "I see them," my brother would say with excitement... "I see them too," I would reply... Despite my claim, the truth was blurred; I never saw a single one. It wasn't long before we discovered my need for glasses— I was nearsighted.

Clarity, like the focus needed to spot animals in the distance, becomes crucial in the terrain of leadership. It helps you cut through uncertainty, offering a clear perspective. Without it, opportunities and challenges, even as large as elephants, remain obscured by the glare.

Navigating the complex world of leadership isn't easy, but having clarity is like having a reliable compass. It cuts through the fog of uncertainty and shows you exactly where to go. It's not just about seeing clearly—it's about knowing your direction and why it matters. When you bring clarity into your leadership style, it helps you make decisions that really count, ones that match your team's goals and give everyone a sense of purpose.

Beyond decision-making, clarity shapes how you talk, act, and connect with others, shaping the very own fabric of organizational culture. Effective communication is key to *EXECUTIVEness*, and when you're crystal clear in your messages, everyone gets it. This kind of communication leaves no room for misinterpretation, nurturing shared understanding and a collective sense of purpose within the team.

So, how can you foster clarity within your leadership?

- Begin by embracing language that speaks to all team members. Simplicity here doesn't imply superficiality—it signifies an in-depth comprehension made accessible.

- Break down complex ideas into manageable components, allowing the entire team to understand and contribute effectively. A leader who champions clarity empowers their team to grasp concepts and work collaboratively toward shared objectives.

- When it comes to strategic undertakings, chart a strategic course considering strengths, obstacles, and aspirations. With clarity you can seamlessly align these elements, providing your team an unobstructed vision of their journey, igniting a sense of purpose and direction that fuels their motivation.

Seven Practical Steps to Foster Clarity:

1. **Define Clear Objectives:** Start by defining specific and measurable goals for your team. Clearly articulate what success looks like and how it will be measured. This clarity sets a focused direction for everyone to follow.

2. **Simplify Communication:** Embrace straightforward language that is accessible to all team members. Avoid jargon or overly complex terms that may confuse or alienate. Break down complex ideas into manageable concepts that everyone can understand.

3. **Encourage Open Dialogue:** Create an environment where team members feel comfortable asking questions and seeking clarification. Foster a culture of transparency where concerns can be addressed openly, promoting mutual understanding.

4. **Provide Context and Purpose:** Help your team understand the broader context behind decisions and initiatives. Clearly communicate how their contributions fit into the larger goals of the organization. This context empowers team members to see the relevance of their work.

5. **Use Visual Aids and Examples:** Utilize visuals, diagrams, or real-life examples to illustrate concepts and ideas. Visual aids can enhance understanding and provide a tangible reference point for discussions.

6. **Regularly Assess Understanding:** Check in with your team regularly to ensure clarity is maintained. Ask for feedback on communication effectiveness and adjust as needed to ensure everyone is on the same page.

7. **Lead by Example:** Demonstrate clarity in your own communication and decision-making. Model the behavior you expect from your team by being clear, concise, and consistent in your interactions.

By implementing these practical steps, you empower your team to navigate challenges with clarity and purpose, fostering a culture where everyone can contribute effectively towards shared objectives.

> CLARITY IN LEADERSHIP IS INVALUABLE. IT CUTS THROUGH NOISE, REVEALS TRUTH, AND TURNS COMPLEXITY INTO ACTIONABLE STEPS.

10.2 Impact: Crafting Leadership with Lasting Influence

Leadership's true measure lies not in fleeting moments but in the lasting influence it leaves behind. As we turn our focus to a new pillar—impact—we explore the art of creating meaningful and enduring change.

Impact isn't about commanding attention through grand gestures. It's about integrating transformative actions into your leadership approach to leave a lasting mark.

Understanding the significance of impact involves recognizing that every decision, every communication sets in motion a chain of events within your leadership landscape. These interactions have the potential to evoke change, inspire innovation, and foster growth.

> TO LEVERAGE ***EXECUTIVENESS*** IN PURSUIT OF IMPACT, COMMIT TO PURPOSEFUL LEADERSHIP. THIS MEANS VIEWING EACH ENDEAVOR THROUGH A LENS OF INTENTIONALITY—ASKING NOT JUST WHAT NEEDS TO BE DONE, BUT WHY AND HOW. THIS PERSPECTIVE COMPELS YOU TO ASSESS YOUR ACTIONS AGAINST A BACKDROP OF LASTING INFLUENCE AND TO CHART A COURSE THAT LEAVES AN INDELIBLE MARK, NOT MERELY TICKS OFF TASKS.

Creating a lasting impact goes beyond immediate outcomes; it's about sculpting a legacy that endures. The techniques to achieve this are as diverse as the scenarios you encounter.

One foundational practice is setting a clear example through your actions. When you align your behavior with the principles you espouse, you forge a path of integrity that others are inspired to follow. This alignment infuses your leadership with authenticity, a quality that resonates deeply and fosters trust.

Another practice is fostering a culture of collaboration. Impact doesn't occur in isolation—it flourishes in an ecosystem of shared ideas, collective effort, and mutual respect. By encouraging your team to contribute their perspectives and insights, you harness the power of diverse thinking, amplifying your capacity for innovative solutions.

Translating impact into tangible outcomes involves strategic thinking. It requires not just addressing present challenges, but also anticipating future needs. When you envision the long-term effects of your decisions and actions, you navigate your team toward sustainable success.

Your potential for impact extends beyond the confines of your immediate environment. The influence you wield is immeasurable. By developing *EXECUTIVEness,* you enhance not only your team's present but also shape a future resonant with your contributions.

Impact is the currency of influential leadership—a testament to your ability to effect meaningful change. As you infuse impact into your leadership, remember that the legacy you leave is a consequence of your deliberate actions, the result of your transformative choices. Through impact, your leadership reverberates through time, echoing your commitment to excellence and shaping the landscape for generations to come.

10.3: The Journey from Clarity and Influence, to Admiration and Respect

Here, we'll explore a crucial transformation in leadership—moving from clarity and influence to earning admiration and respect.

From Clarity to Respect

Let me illustrate this point with a story about one of my clients, Fernando, a manager who embodied *EXECUTIVEness* during the tumultuous days of the pandemic.

As workplaces were transformed and challenges multiplied, Fernando's leadership stood out as a beacon of unwavering clarity, influence, and genuine care.

Amidst the chaos, Fernando understood that in times of crisis, clarity of purpose and vision becomes even more vital. By consistently communicating a clear and compassionate message about the company's commitment to its employees' well-being, he instilled trust and confidence.

But Fernando's clarity wasn't confined to words alone; it was mirrored in his actions. He was resolute in his dedication to preserving jobs and supporting his team. In a bold move, he volunteered to take a significant pay cut to show solidarity and support for his employees, proving that his leadership principles were backed by tangible actions.

Furthermore, Fernando recognized the challenges faced by parents working from home with children. He responded by sending tablets loaded with games and educational activities to every member of his team. This meaningful gesture provided practical relief and fostered a sense of camaraderie and understanding.

What truly set Fernando apart was his consistency in delivering on his promises. As the pandemic persisted, he continued to adapt schedules, offer support, and find innovative solutions to emerging challenges. This steadfast alignment of actions with the company's vision cultivated an atmosphere of respect and admiration among his team members and beyond.

Bringing Vision to Life

Vision isn't just a lofty concept; it's a blueprint for transformation and progress. Leaders who articulate their vision with clarity and conviction possess a magnetic quality that draws others in. When communicated transparently and sincerely, your vision becomes a rallying call for action—a shared purpose that unites the team.

The Power of Execution

Transitioning from vision to admiration requires more than words—it demands translating intentions into actionable steps that drive change. Effective leaders ensure their vision isn't just aspirational but executable. Dedication to execution, commitment to promises, and resilience in overcoming obstacles build credibility and trust.

Cultivating Respect through Consistency

Respect isn't freely given; it's earned through consistent actions aligned with your vision. From influence to admiration, demonstrating unwavering values, ethics, and principles creates a foundation of trust. Consistently prioritizing team well-being and growth fosters enduring respect.

Earning Admiration through Extraordinary Acts

Admiration stems from leaders who go beyond the call of duty. Acts of genuine care during challenges—supporting personal struggles, accommodating unique needs—demonstrate empathy and foster admiration. These extraordinary gestures leave a lasting impact and solidify a leader's reputation as someone who genuinely cares.

> THE JOURNEY FROM CLARITY AND INFLUENCE, TO RESPECT AND ADMIRATION IS CONTINUOUS. YOUR ABILITY TO CONSISTENTLY DELIVER ON PROMISES, RESPOND WITH EMPATHY TO CHANGE, AND CULTIVATE MUTUAL RESPECT REINFORCES YOUR ROLE AS AN INSPIRATIONAL LEADER. THIS JOURNEY CULMINATES IN A LEGACY OF SUPERIOR LEADERSHIP, LEAVING AN INDELIBLE MARK ON THOSE YOU LEAD.

10.4: Translating Principles into Action: From Theory to Tangible Impact

As we close this chapter, let's solidify Your journey by transforming these insights into everyday practices.

Exercise: Clarity and Influence Reflection

Take a moment to review recent instances where your clarity of purpose and influential actions intersected. Reflect on how these instances generated admiration and respect from your team or peers. Identify specific behaviors, decisions, or communication strategies that contributed to this outcome. Consider how you can replicate these behaviors in future interactions to consistently foster admiration and respect.

Exercise: Authenticity in Action

Choose a scenario where you can embody the principles of clarity and influence to inspire admiration and respect. Craft a concise plan outlining your intended actions, ensuring they align with your vision and values. Execute this plan with a focus on authenticity – be genuine and transparent in your approach. After the interaction, reflect on the impact your actions had on generating admiration and respect.

Exercise: The Ripple Effect Challenge

Identify a goal you'd like to achieve within your team or organization. Implement consistent actions aligned with *EXECUTIVEness* principles to progress towards this goal. Document your journey, recording both successes and challenges along the way. This exercise helps you witness the ripple effect of clarity, influence, and purpose as they culminate in respect and admiration over time.

Exercise: Reflect and Refine

Regularly set aside time for self-reflection. Review your recent interactions, decisions, and actions through the lens of *EXECUTIVEness.* Ask yourself: How did clarity, influence, purpose, and respect manifest in my leadership today? Note instances where you excelled and areas where improvement is possible. This practice fosters ongoing self-awareness and ensures your commitment to actionable leadership.

These exercises enable you to infuse these principles into your daily leadership interactions. By consistently applying these practices, you'll witness how clarity, influence, purpose, and respect seamlessly blend to create a leadership style that garners admiration and respect, promoting a positive impact on those around you. Through deliberate action, you transform concepts into reality, making *EXECUTIVEness* an integral part of your journey.

Navigating the Path Ahead

As we shift our focus towards the future of leadership, we find ourselves at a crucial crossroads where transformation and potential intersect.

In the chapters ahead, we'll discuss critical subjects such as globalization, diversity, inclusion, the ever-changing realm of technology, and the intricate art of leading in a VUCA (Volatile, Uncertain, Complex, Ambiguous) world. Each of these elements contributes to a panoramic understanding of the evolving leadership landscape, presenting both opportunities and obstacles that demand our careful consideration.

The chapters are designed to equip you for the path ahead—a path that demands adaptability, resilience, and a forward-looking mindset. As we engage with these topics, it's important to recognize that our leadership's potency lies not solely in our present knowledge, but also in our ability to envision, innovate, and lead with a lasting impact.

Chapter 11:

Continuity and Progress: Navigating the Evolving Landscape

In the rapidly evolving landscape of today's workplaces, the influence of diversity and inclusion takes center stage, bringing both, opportunities and challenges. We're at a point where tradition meets change, where core values and beliefs intersect with a diverse workforce. What makes this particularly unique is that five distinct generations are working together, a phenomenon that highlights the immense potential of cross-generational interactions.

This convergence is a product of the remarkable progress we've made in extending both the quality and length of our lives. As a result, the once-clear boundaries between generations have blurred, giving rise to an unprecedented coexistence of Baby Boomers, Gen X, Millennials, Gen Z, and members of the Silent Generation. This merging marks a shift in the way work is perceived and requires a recalibration of leadership approaches to embrace the diversity that defines teams.

In this chapter, we dive into the complex connections between values, beliefs, and multi-generational collaboration. Our exploration aims to understand the details of this collaboration and navigate the unfamiliar territory of this transformative era. We'll leverage the principles of *EXECUTIVEness* to shed light onto this new blend of talents.

11.1 Embracing Growth: Navigating Continuous Evolution in Leadership

The Essence of a Growth Mindset:

The term growth mindset represents the belief that one's abilities and intelligence can be developed and improved with time, through hard work, commitment, learning, and perseverance.

If you find yourself believing that you can always learn from your experiences, challenges, and failures, that you IQ is not a set number, and view challenges as paths to improvement rather than obstacles, you may lean towards a Growth Mindset. However, belief alone isn't sufficient. Putting this mindset into action is crucial. If you catch yourself dismissing opportunities with thought like "I'm too old" or "that's not for me", it's time to actively practice a Growth Mindeset or to re-examine your point of view.

When you adopt and act upon this perspective, you see challenges as opportunities, and failures as chances to learn and improve, consequently fostering a culture of continuous self-challenge and growth. A growth mindset not only encourages adaptability and proactivity in learning but also nurtures resilience, a readiness to tackle challenges, and the realization that setbacks are stepping stones on your path to growth. This mindset instills a thirst for knowledge, an eagerness to adapt and change, and a willingness to take risks.

Why a Growth Mindset Matters in Leadership:

Leaders who possess a growth mindset thrive in today's fast-paced and ever-evolving business environment. Their willingness to step out of their comfort zones, learn new skills, and adapt to changing circumstances fosters innovation and resilience. This mindset encourages leaders to seek out diverse experiences, push their limits, and constantly seek improvement, enabling them to navigate complexities with agility and confidence.

A Personal Journey of Evolution:

A pivotal moment in my career unfolded when I transitioned from the role of Director of Sales to venture into Marketing, driven by the desire for a better work-life balance.

Throughout my journey, I took calculated risks, kept improving, and stayed driven to succeed. Change pushed me trust the mindset I'd honed over the years—one that sees adapting as essential and views instability as a constant companion.

With an openness to change, a readiness to adapt, and a keen awareness that my journey was an evolving narrative, I didn't see this new direction as a complete shift, just a different route to the same goals.

During this time of self-reinvention, I really began to appreciate the power of the "growth mindset" I'd developed. It gave me the confidence to manage transitions without fear or self-imposed limits.

There were plenty of moments that showed how my belief in growth played out—some were triumphs, and others, well, were more like less-that-gracious stumbles. But let's be honest, growth isn't always a smooth journey. And that's okay; it's just part of the messy, but rewarding, dance of personal and professional growth.

My journey was marked by measured risks, continuous improvement, and an unyielding drive to succeed. I knew that a growth mindset demands embracing change, evolving, and propelling oneself and others forward even in unfamiliar territories.

Cultivating a Growth Mindset in Leadership:

To cultivate a growth mindset, you can start by acknowledging the potential for growth and change. Embrace challenges as opportunities to gain experience and improve, encourage your team members to take risks and innovate, and create an environment where learning is celebrated.

By adopting a growth mindset culture, you not only inspire individual growth but also elevate the collective capacity of the team to tackle complex problems and seize new possibilities.

> AS YOU JOURNEY THROUGH THE CONCEPT OF CONTINUOUS EVOLUTION, REMEMBER THAT A GROWTH MINDSET ISN'T JUST A CATCHPHRASE—IT'S A MINDSET THAT HAS THE POTENTIAL TO RESHAPE YOUR LEADERSHIP APPROACH, DRIVE INNOVATION, AND CREATE A CULTURE OF LEARNING AND ADAPTATION.

11.2: Navigating Globalization and Generational Diversity in Leadership

In today's interconnected world, the boundaries of the workplace have expanded beyond geographical borders. Globalization has brought with it a diverse workforce, rich in cultural, generational, and experiential differences. We're at a point where core values and beliefs intersect with a diverse workforce. In this chapter, let's look at the complexities and opportunities that arise from navigating this new global and diverse landscape.

Understanding the Global Tapestry:

The influence of globalization on leadership cannot be underestimated. As organizations operate across different time zones, cultures, and languages, leaders must develop a global perspective. *EXECUTIVEness* principles enable leaders to transcend cultural differences, fostering a climate of collaboration and innovation across borders.

In the global landscape of leadership, *EXECUTIVEness* serves as a guiding force, helping leaders navigate the complexity of diverse cultures, perspectives, and experiences. As organizations expand their reach across borders, leaders face the challenge of coordinating teams comprised of individuals from all corners of the world. In this intricate collaborative journey, open-mindedness becomes the compass that steers the ship.

EXECUTIVEness urges leaders to shatter the confines of their own cultural lens and embrace the richness of global diversity. It fosters an environment where differences are celebrated and leveraged as assets. This approach doesn't merely acknowledge diversity—it cultivates a genuine curiosity about others' viewpoints and experiences. It's about recognizing that solutions and strategies are enriched when they're born from a tapestry of cultural influences.

Active listening, a cornerstone of *EXECUTIVEness*, becomes your bridge that connects you with your team members' stories, concerns, and aspirations. In a global landscape, understanding transcends language; it's about deciphering the nuances of unspoken cues, acknowledging the emotions behind words, and attuning to the unique perspectives that shape each team member's approach.

Empathetic leadership, another hallmark of *EXECUTIVEness*, becomes the glue to bind a diverse team together. Empathy isn't confined to understanding someone's feelings—it's about walking in their shoes, experiencing their challenges, and celebrating their triumphs. In a global context, empathy becomes your tool to dismantle barriers, fostering a sense of unity and camaraderie across cultural divides.

EXECUTIVEness encourages you to operate as global citizens—as an individual who is deeply attuned to the myriad cultures that converge within your world. By embracing open-mindedness, active listening, and empathetic leadership, you create a fertile ground where ideas flourish, creativity thrives, and collaboration knows no bounds.

Five Generations United:

For the first time in history, five distinct generations coexist in today's workforce, each bringing unique values, communication styles, and expectations. This convergence is a testament to our extended quality of life, blurring once-clear generational boundaries and necessitating a recalibration of leadership approaches to embrace diversity within teams.

> *EXECUTIVENESS* EQUIPS LEADERS TO CREATE AN INCLUSIVE ENVIRONMENT THAT BRIDGES GENERATIONAL GAPS AND CAPITALIZES ON THE STRENGTHS OF EACH COHORT.

Today's workforce is a mosaic of generations, each contributing distinct perspectives, values, and approaches. From the seasoned wisdom of Baby Boomers to the tech-savvy innovation of Gen Z, these generational dynamics shape the fabric of organizations. Understanding these cohorts is crucial for harnessing their collective wisdom to drive creativity and productivity.

- **Baby Boomers**, shaped by post-war optimism, bring experience and a strong work ethic. They offer invaluable mentorship and institutional knowledge.

- **Gen X**, known for independence and adaptability, bridge analog and digital eras with pragmatic critical thinking skills and resilience to change.

- **Millennials**, driven by purpose and digital fluency, inject fresh perspectives and innovative ideas. They prioritize work-life balance and seek meaningful impact.

- **Gen Z**, as digital natives, possess innate understanding of technology and social media, making them agile in digital environments.

These snapshots highlight samples of their unique generic characteristics, simple examples of their collective strength in collaborative settings.

EXECUTIVEness empowers leaders to leverage generational strengths and foster an inclusive culture that bridges potential gaps. By tapping into diverse experiences, organizations can promote collaboration that leads to innovative solutions.

It encourages cultivating a culture of continuous learning across all generations, nurturing an environment where generational wisdom merges to drive innovation and enhance productivity.

BY EMBRACING THE UNIQUE ATTRIBUTES OF
MULTIPLE GENERATIONS, LEADERS CAN CULTIVATE
AN ENVIRONMENT WHERE INTERGENERATIONAL
COLLABORATION THRIVES. THIS FUSION OF WISDOM
AND INNOVATION PROPELS ORGANIZATIONS TOWARD
SUCCESS IN AN INCREASINGLY DIVERSE AND DYNAMIC
WORLD.

Embracing Diversity in All Forms:

In today's interconnected world, diversity manifests in myriad ways, encompassing cultural backgrounds, religious beliefs, gender identities, physical abilities, and many other characteristics. Recognizing and embracing this rich tapestry of diversity is essential for fostering an inclusive and supportive environment.

Understanding and respecting the diverse aspects that define individuals is crucial. *EXECUTIVEness* promotes an ethos where differences are celebrated, ensuring that every individual feels valued and respected.

By fostering sensitivity and inclusivity, leaders cultivate an environment where diverse perspectives thrive, enriching collaboration and innovation. Embracing diversity in all its forms not only strengthens organizational culture but also enhances collective creativity and problem-solving abilities.

Practical Strategies for Inclusive Leadership:

Effective leadership demands a nuanced understanding of diversity and inclusion. It's about balancing local customs with a cohesive organizational culture. *EXECUTIVEness* provides a roadmap to navigate this complexity, ensuring that diverse teams feel valued and empowered.

Embracing Inclusive Leadership:

Today's inclusive leadership goes beyond tolerance; it's about actively understanding, embracing, and leveraging differences to drive organizational success. EXECUTIVEness principles empower leaders to foster unity amid diversity.

Empathy in Action:

Empathy is foundational to inclusive leadership. By understanding and appreciating the unique perspectives and challenges of team members, leaders can tailor their interactions to create an environment where every voice is heard and valued. For example, actively listening to diverse viewpoints and addressing concerns with sensitivity fosters trust and inclusivity.

Adaptability and Flexibility:

In a global context, adaptability is key. Leaders must be agile in accommodating diverse cultural norms and practices while upholding organizational values. This requires a willingness to challenge biases and learn from diverse cultural perspectives. For instance, adjusting communication styles or team practices to align with local customs promotes a sense of belonging and mutual respect.

Open-Minded Collaboration:

Open-mindedness bridges diverse perspectives, sparking innovation and mutual understanding. *EXECUTIVEness* encourages leaders to embrace innovative ideas and approaches, fostering cross-cultural learning and creativity within teams. By creating opportunities for diverse team members to contribute their insights, leaders cultivate an inclusive culture of innovation and growth.

Promoting a Culture of Inclusion:

Setting clear expectations for respectful communication, valuing diverse opinions, and fostering cross-cultural collaboration are essential to promoting inclusion. Leaders can actively create opportunities for team members to apply their unique strengths and contribute meaningfully to organizational goals.

> LEADERS WHO AUTHENTICALLY PRACTICE EMP-ATHY, ADAPTABILITY, AND OPEN-MINDEDNESS CAN BRIDGE CULTURAL GAPS, SUPPORT INCLUSIVITY, AND DRIVE SUSTAINABLE SUCCESS WHERE DIVERSITY IS CELEBRATED AND LEVERAGED AS A STRATEGIC ADVANTAGE.

11.3: Leading with Clarity and Impact through Continuous Growth

In today's dynamic business landscape, work and business is in a constant state of flux. Technological advancements, global economic shifts, and societal changes all contribute to an environment that demands adaptability and foresight from leaders. To effectively lead amidst these complexities, it's crucial to address key shifts that are shaping the future of work and business.

Workforce Evolution:

The composition of the workforce is undergoing a significant transformation. As the Baby Boomer generation gradually retires, we are witnessing the rise of Generation Z and the continued presence of Millennials. This generational mix brings diverse perspectives, expectations, and work styles. *EXECUTIVEness* emphasizes the importance of creating an inclusive environment that values and harnesses this diversity for increased creativity and productivity.

Rapid Technological Changes:

Technological innovations, especially in the realm of artificial intelligence and automation, are reshaping industries. Leaders need to understand how these changes can disrupt traditional roles and workflows. *EXECUTIVEness* encourages you to adopt a growth mindset, fostering a continuous learning culture that equips teams to adapt to new technologies and take advantage of emerging opportunities.

Globalization and Connectivity:

The world is more interconnected than ever before, resulting in a global marketplace that transcends geographical boundaries. Leaders must consider cultural nuances, varying business practices, and diverse customer bases. *EXECUTIVEness* stresses the value of open-mindedness and empathy, and effective cross-cultural communication and collaboration.

Environmental and Social Responsibility:

Organizations are increasingly expected to operate in environmentally and socially responsible ways. Sustainability and ethical business practices are gaining prominence. *EXECUTIVEness* prompts you to align your values with your leadership approach, ensuring that decisions and actions contribute to positive societal and environmental impacts.

Tools for Navigating Change:

To thrive, leaders can draw upon tools and strategies. Embracing ongoing learning and professional development helps you stay current with industry trends and evolving best practices. *EXECUTIVEness* emphasizes self-awareness and adaptability, enabling you to identify their strengths and areas for growth and adjust your approach as needed.

Maintaining a Growth Mindset:

The essence of *EXECUTIVEness* lies in a growth mindset – a willingness to see change and view challenges as opportunities for growth. Leaders should encourage this mindset among their teams, fostering a culture where curiosity, innovation, and resilience are celebrated.

Navigating the Shifting Landscape:

As you chart our course through this shifting landscape, *EXECUTIVEness* equips you to be an agile leader who thrives amidst uncertainty. By leveraging self-awareness, adaptability, and a growth mindset, you not only steer your teams through change but also create a lasting impact in the face of evolving challenges and opportunities.

11.4 Leading with Purpose: A Mindful Approach to Impactful Leadership

In the realm of leadership, the pursuit of success extends beyond mere profit and performance. It's about embracing purpose as a driving force. *EXECUTIVEness* encourages an introspective journey that reveals the intrinsic motivations and values that guide leaders toward meaningful impact.

> LEADING WITH PURPOSE ISN'T A SUPERFICIAL PURSUIT; RATHER, IT'S A HOLISTIC APPROACH THAT TRANSFORMS PEOPLE, FOSTERS AUTHENTICITY, AND SHAPES ORGANIZATIONAL CULTURE.

Discovering Deeper Purpose:

EXECUTIVEness gives you the tools to explore inner motivations – the driving forces that push you beyond the ordinary. When you discover your intrinsic purpose, you become a source of inspiration, motivating others to connect their efforts to a larger mission.

For instance, if you're passionate about environmental sustainability, integrating this purpose into your leadership can inspire your team to adopt eco-friendly practices, creating a culture of environmental responsibility within the organization.

Aligning Actions with Values:

Purpose-driven leadership is rooted in integrity and consistency. *EXECUTIVEness* calls for leaders to align their actions with their personal values and the greater good. This alignment isn't just a surface-level practice; it resonates deeply with teams and stakeholders, creating a foundation of trust and respect.

Imagine yourself valuing transparency and open communication. By consistently practicing these values in your interactions, you establish a culture of honesty and collaboration within the team. This, in turn, leads to smoother workflows, improved problem-solving, and enhanced employee satisfaction.

Creating Lasting Impact:

Impactful leadership transcends immediate results; it's about planting the seeds of positive change that endure over time. *EXECUTIVEness* encourages leaders to think beyond short-term achievements and focus on the long-lasting legacy they leave behind.

By investing in the growth and development of those around you, you are not just leaving a mark, you are creating a lasting legacy. By investing in the growth and development of those around you, you create a lasting legacy. This enduring impact, fostered through opportunities for skill enhancement and career advancement, ensures that individuals empowered to thrive carry forward your influence long after you've moved on. It's a legacy of profound significance, a testament to the supreme importance of leadership that shapes enduring success.

Fostering a Culture of Purpose:

Leadership with purpose ripples throughout an organization, influencing its culture and dynamics. *EXECUTIVEness* emphasizes clear communication of purpose, creating an environment where every team member understands how their work contributes to a larger vision.

How can you achieve that? Effectively communicate the specific tasks assigned to each role, elucidating how these contribute to tangible outcomes within the department. Align these outcomes with the broader objectives of the company, forging a clear link between individual responsibilities and the organization's overarching goals.

By fostering this connection, team members understand how their daily efforts are integral to achieving the company's mission. This deliberate alignment of tasks, roles, outcomes and purpose not only instills a sense of significance in each team member but also forms the foundation for a cohesive and purpose-driven organizational culture.

Navigating Challenges with Purpose:

Challenges are inevitable in the journey of leadership, and purpose serves as a guiding light. Purpose, as many of the other aspects of *EXECUTIVEness* we discussed, equips you with the resilience to view obstacles as opportunities for growth. A purpose-driven leader applies this mindset to challenges, encouraging their team and organization to approach difficulties as steppingstones toward improvement.

For instance, consider yourself navigating a market disruption. Instead of succumbing to panic and opting to retract and observe, understanding and embracing your and your organization's purpose, you will be equipped to inspire your team to innovate, adapt, and find creative solutions that not only weather the storm but position the organization for future success.

Crafting Your Leadership Legacy:

Leading with purpose isn't a single action; it's a continuous commitment that transforms leaders into catalysts of positive change. *EXECUTIVEness* fuels an intentional and mindful approach to leadership that resonates far beyond immediate outcomes. By aligning actions with values, communicating purpose clearly, and fostering a culture of shared dedication, you create a legacy of purpose-driven influence.

11.5 Translating *EXECUTIVEness* into Action: Navigating the Evolving Landscape

Now, let's translate these insights into actionable steps that empower you to navigate the evolving landscape with clarity, purpose, and impact:

Exercise: Continuity of Growth

Reflect on your leadership journey and the concept of continuous growth. Identify areas where you've embraced change and growth, and pinpoint instances where your mindset shifted to adapt to evolving circumstances. Set a goal to consistently seek opportunities for growth in both your leadership approach and personal development.

Exercise: Global Mindset Reflection

Consider your experiences in a global context, whether through diverse teams, cross-border collaborations, or multicultural interactions. Reflect on moments where a global mindset enriched your decision-making or communication. Develop a plan to further cultivate a global perspective, such as engaging in cross-cultural conversations or seeking insights from international leaders.

Exercise: Purpose-Driven Action

Take stock of your leadership actions and assess how they align with your purpose and values. Identify instances where your actions resonated with your purpose, driving a positive impact on your team or organization. Craft a clear plan to infuse purpose into your leadership style, consistently aligning your decisions and actions with your overarching mission.

Exercise: Clarity in Action

Reflect on recent interactions where you communicated with clarity and impact. Consider how these instances influenced others and contributed to a shared understanding of goals. Set a goal to consistently communicate with clarity, whether in team discussions, strategic planning, or individual interactions. Monitor the outcomes of these clear communications and adjust your approach as needed.

As you navigate this dynamic journey, remember that each step you take brings you closer to your vision of impactful leadership.

Chapter 12:

Navigating the Technological Landscape: Leadership in the Digital Age

Let's explore now the intersection of leadership and technology and how leaders can navigate the digital landscape, leverage technological trends, and integrate digital tools to drive impactful results.

12.1 The Digital Transformation Imperative: Understanding the Role of Technology in Modern Leadership

The Digital Disruption:

The digital revolution has disrupted entire industries, altering how businesses operate and how leaders must lead. For instance, consider Kodak, a company that once dominated the photography industry but failed to adapt to the digital era. Despite inventing the digital camera, Kodak clung to its traditional film-based business model. This lack of adaptability led to its downfall as digital photography became the new norm.

Acknowledging the perpetual nature of technological change is paramount. You must not only be agile in your responses but also, adopt an initiative-taking stance by exploring scenarios where technology can either assist, replace or entirely transform your organization. Failing to do so may leave you vulnerable to the disruptive forces that have led to the downfall of once-thriving companies. Embracing change and staying ahead in the digital realm is not just a strategy; it's a prerequisite for sustained success in the modern business environment.

Adapt or Lag Behind:

The choice for leaders is clear: adapt or risk falling behind. Blockbuster is a classic example of a company that didn't adapt. At its peak, Blockbuster was synonymous with video rentals. However, it failed to pivot as streaming services like Netflix emerged. Blockbuster's inability to foresee the digital shift and adapt accordingly led to its bankruptcy. Effective leaders must be proactive in embracing technological change to ensure their organizations' survival. Embracing change and staying ahead in the digital realm is not just a strategy; it's a prerequisite for sustained success in the modern business environment.

Creating Digital-First Organizations:

Organizations like Amazon, Netflix, and Tesla have become pioneers in the digital-first approach. Amazon transformed from an online bookseller into an e-commerce giant and cloud computing leader. Netflix reinvented the way we consume entertainment, shifting from DVDs to streaming. Tesla revolutionized the automotive industry by prioritizing electric vehicles and software integration. These companies exemplify how leaders can create digital-first cultures that drive innovation and success.

Case Studies:

In this section, we'll delve into these case studies in more detail. For instance, we'll examine how Netflix transitioned from a DVD rental service to a content production powerhouse by leveraging data and digital technology. We'll also explore how Tesla's electric cars and software updates have disrupted the automotive industry. These cases provide actionable insights for leaders looking to navigate the digital age effectively.

Before delving into these case studies, it's important to clarify that this is not an endorsement to these companies and their business. Rather, these examples serve as illustrations of how certain organizations navigated and, in some cases, pioneered transformative shifts in their industries. The intention is to emphasize how they overcame challenges and demonstrate visionary leadership in recognizing and capitalizing on emerging possibilities.

Amazon: From Bookseller to E-commerce Behemoth

Amazon's journey from a modest online bookstore to one of the world's largest e-commerce and cloud computing companies is a remarkable example of digital transformation. Key points to consider:

The Digital Evolution: *Amazon's founder, Jeff Bezos, recognized the potential of the internet early on and expanded beyond bookselling into various product categories. He embraced the digital landscape to create an online marketplace that offered convenience, variety, and competitive pricing.*

Data-Driven Decision Making: *Amazon's success is heavily driven by its data-centric approach. The company collects vast amounts of customer data to personalize recommendations and improve the user experience. Leaders at Amazon understand the* importance of data analytics and use it to drive innovation and decision-making.

Cloud Computing Revolution: Amazon Web Services (AWS) is a prime example of how Amazon leveraged its infrastructure and technical expertise to offer cloud computing services. AWS revolutionized the tech industry and positioned Amazon as a leader in the cloud computing space.

Netflix: Redefining Entertainment with Streaming

Netflix's transformation from a DVD rental service to a global streaming powerhouse illustrates the power of adapting to technological shifts. Key points to explore:

Recognizing Market Trends: Netflix anticipated the decline of physical media and identified the potential of streaming technology. By offering a convenient, on-demand streaming service, it revolutionized the way people consume entertainment.

Original Content Strategy: Netflix's shift towards producing original content, like "House of Cards" and "Stranger Things," marked a pivotal moment in its growth. By using data to identify viewer preferences, Netflix created content that resonated with its audience.

Global Expansion: Netflix expanded its reach worldwide, embracing globalization as a means of growth. It recognized the value of content localization to cater to diverse markets.

Tesla: Disrupting the Automotive Industry with Electric Vehicles

Tesla's innovative approach to the automotive industry demonstrates how a company can leverage technology to redefine a traditional sector. Key insights to consider:

Electric Vehicle Revolution: *Tesla recognized the potential of electric vehicles when many believed they were impractical. By combining electric power with cutting-edge technology, Tesla created high-performance electric cars that challenged the dominance of internal combustion engines.*

Software Integration: *Tesla's unique ability to update vehicle software remotely has allowed the company to continuously improve its vehicles' performance, safety features, and user experience. This approach sets Tesla apart in the automotive industry.*

Sustainability and Future Vision: *Beyond electric vehicles, Tesla has ventured into renewable energy solutions and a vision of a sustainable future. Its focus on environmental responsibility aligns with the changing expectations of consumers.*

These case studies serve as powerful illustrations of how embracing digital transformation, harnessing technology, and employing innovative strategies can lead to triumphant success in a rapidly evolving world. They highlight both the risks of not adapting to digital transformation and the rewards of embracing it. Keeping awareness at the forefront of your decision-making will empower you to make informed choices and lead your organization into a more technologically advanced future.

The Impact of *EXECUTIVEness*:

- **Visionary Leadership:** *EXECUTIVEness* encourages you to envision a future unburdened by preconceived notions, similar to how Netflix envisioned a world without DVDs. It prompts you to set bold, transformative goals, such as Tesla's mission to electrify the automotive industry. By aligning you vision with their organization's values and leveraging technology, you can ignite the spark of innovation and drive meaningful change.

- **Data-Informed Decision-Making:** In the digital age, data reigns supreme. Amazon's relentless pursuit of data-driven insights underscores the importance of informed decision-making. As a superior leader, harness data to understand market trends, customer preferences, and operational efficiency. Recognize that data isn't just a tool; it's a strategic asset that fuels progress.

- **Agility and Adaptability:** Just as Tesla adapted its electric vehicle technology, *EXECUTIVEness* fosters adaptability. You must be agile in responding to market shifts, emerging technologies, and changing consumer expectations. Flexibility is a hallmark of leadership in the digital era.

- **Ethical Considerations:** In the pursuit of technological innovation, leaders should never lose sight of ethics. Tesla's commitment to sustainability exemplifies how values can shape an organization's direction. Think about and prioritize ethical conduct, ensuring that your technological advancements align with societal values and don't compromise integrity.

Indicators for Change:

- **Market Disruption:** Disruptions in your industry, similar to the rise of e-commerce or streaming services, can be a compelling signal for change. When fresh players or technologies alter the competitive landscape, it's essential to reassess your strategies.

- **Customer Expectations:** Shifts in customer preferences and behaviors, often influenced by technology, demand responsive leadership. If your audience expects digital interactions, personalized experiences, or innovative solutions, these are obvious signs that it's time to adapt.

- **Technological Advancements:** Keeping a pulse on technological trends, like the growth of AI, automation, or remote work tools, is vital. Leaders who fail to integrate relevant technology risk falling behind their competitors.

- **Environmental and Social Factors:** As the world becomes more interconnected, environmental and social responsibility play an increasing role in leadership. Leaders who disregard sustainability, diversity, and social impact risk alienating stakeholders and damaging their reputation.

> ***EXECUTIVENESS*** DEMANDS YOU TO PROACTIVELY EMBRACE CHANGE, SEIZE OPPORTUNITIES, AND LEAD THEIR ORGANIZATIONS INTO A FUTURE BRIMMING WITH TECHNOLOGICAL POSSIBILITIES.

12.2 The Phases of Technological Evolution: A Historical Perspective

Technological progress often follows an exponential curve. Imagine a graph where progress starts slowly and gradually but then accelerates dramatically, resulting in rapid and significant changes over a brief period.

Phases of Technological Evolution

- **Agricultural Era (Lasted approximately 8,000 years):** This era marked the beginning of human civilization, where people transitioned from nomadic hunting and gathering to settled farming. It laid the foundation for societal structures, culture, and organized communities. Leaders of this era focused on resource management and community building.

- **Industrial Revolution (Lasted approximately 100 years):** The Industrial Revolution brought about mechanization, factories, and mass production. This period drastically altered economies, leading to urbanization and significant social changes. Leaders during this era had to adapt to new manufacturing methods, labor relations, and global trade.

- **Information Age (Lasted approximately 60 years):** The advent of computers and the internet transformed how information was processed and shared. This era saw the rise of knowledge workers, increased connectivity, and the emergence of the digital economy. Leaders needed to harness technology for productivity and innovation.

- **Digital Era (Last 30 years):** The Digital Era, which has spanned the last three decades, has been characterized by the proliferation of digital technologies, data-driven decision-making, and the rise of automation and artificial intelligence. The need for resilience and adaptability became strikingly evident in recent years as we swiftly adapted to entirely new work models.

- **Entering the Next Chapter (An Era Yet to Be Defined):** As we stand at the precipice of the future, we find ourselves at the end of the Digital Era, a period marked by the widespread adoption of digital technologies and data-driven decision-making. The digital tools and platforms we once marveled at have matured, and new frontiers beckon.

The question that looms before us is, "What comes next?" Will it be the era of **Artificial Intelligence (AI)**, where machines take on increasingly complex tasks and decision-making is augmented by algorithms? Or it will be the **Biotechnology Age,** marked by advancements in healthcare, genetic engineering, and life sciences? Alternatively, we may find ourselves in the **Space Age**, exploring the cosmos and expanding our presence beyond Earth.

Whatever the next chapter holds, one thing is certain: it will demand unparalleled adaptability and a steadfast growth mindset from leaders who guide the workforce and shape the future.

12.3 Embracing Technological Trends: Insights into the Future of Work

Keep this in mind: To excel in the business world you must be extremely familiar with the technological trends shaping the way we work. These trends are not mere buzzwords; they carry immense significance for leadership and organizational success.

AI, once relegated to science fiction, has become a powerful tool. Leaders need to recognize AI's potential in automating routine tasks, analyzing vast datasets, and offering valuable insights. The application of AI can significantly enhance operational efficiency by reducing manual workloads, enhance decision-making by providing data-driven insights, and open doors to new opportunities through predictive analytics.

Automation is also revolutionizing the way work gets done. It's imperative for leaders to pinpoint areas where automation can be employed. By automating repetitive tasks, leaders can empower their teams to focus on high-value, creative work. This not only leads to improved productivity and reduced errors but also enables teams to adapt to more dynamic roles.

We have to recognize that the COVID-19 pandemic functioned as a catalyst for technology adoption. We rapidly adopted video conferencing for work and social purposes, Tele Medicine consultations became widespread practice, and online order and delivery became essential.

Leaders adapted to effectively managing remote teams, ensuring seamless collaboration through digital platforms, nurturing employee well-being, and exploiting digital tools for transparent and efficient communication. This continuous adaptation is not just about embracing remote work; it's about fostering a culture of trust and accountability surpassing physical and geographic location.

And all of this requires data. Not only collecting, translating and interpreting data, but uncovering hidden insights that drive informed decision-making is where the true power of data lies.

Consider an example from the retail sector.

A small retail home goods chain noticed a decline in sales in one of its stores, and initial data analysis showed a drop in foot traffic as a probable cause. However, as we dug deeper dive into the data, it revealed something intriguing. Sales of certain high-margin products, like premium coffee machines, had remained consistent, even increasing slightly.

This unexpected insight prompted further investigation. The leadership team decided to analyze customer transaction data and discovered that a sizable number of customers who had purchased these premium coffee machines had also bought expensive coffee beans and accessories. This indicated that the store had attracted a niche market of coffee enthusiasts willing to spend more on complementary products. Digging deeper, overlaying demographic, psychographic and other behavioral data, we were able to identify a new customer avatar.

Armed with this knowledge, strategic changes were made. They decided to redesign the store layout, create a dedicated section for premium coffee-related products and expand their book and gifts selection. They also introduced regular coffee-tasting events and workshops and developed a simple app for customers to track new product launches, register for events and more.

The results were remarkable. Not only did foot traffic rebound, but they also attracted a new customer base. The store's revenue soared as the niche market's presence grew. The store became a destination for coffee lovers, thanks to the leadership team's ability to explore data and uncover insights beyond the surface-level analysis and integrate digital tools to their marketing strategy.

It's not enough to rely on superficial data analysis; you must cultivate the ability to dig deeper, question assumptions, and uncover hidden opportunities or challenges, in essence, practice your *EXECUTIVEness.*

Data exploration allows leaders to identify unconventional patterns. Sometimes, the most valuable insights emerge from patterns that defy conventional wisdom. Data exploration helps leaders spot these anomalies and determine whether they represent untapped opportunities or risks.

> DATA EXPLORATION IS A CRITICAL SKILL FOR LEADERS IN THE DIGITAL AGE. IT GOES BEYOND BASIC DATA INTERPRETATION, ENABLING LEADERS TO UNCOVER HIDDEN OPPORTUNITIES AND MAKE DATADRIVEN DECISIONS THAT IMPACT THE BOTTOM LINE POSITIVELY.

Navigating the Future: Preparing for Tomorrow's Challenges

Peering into the future, leaders must consider how emerging technological trends will mold the workplace and leadership practices. These trends carry profound implications that effective leaders need to acknowledge and address.

As AI continues to advance, it will play an ever-increasing role in decision-making processes. As a leader, you must understand the capabilities and limitations of AI to ensure that decisions align with organizational objectives and values. This involves a strategic approach to incorporating AI into decision-making, where human judgment and ethical considerations guide AI-driven insights.

I believe this new automation wave may lead to rapid workforce transformations. Reskilling and upskilling initiatives, to equip employees with the necessary skills to remain relevant in an evolving job market will be expected from those in leadership positions, ensuring the workforce adapts to these changes is pivotal for the organization's sustainability and growth.

Initiating re-skilling and up-skilling initiatives now, to equip employees with the essential skill for an evolving job market is imperative for your success, your teams' success and the success of your organization. Waiting is not an option, anticipating and adapting to changes in roles, especially with increasing integration of AI, is key for the organizations' sustainability and growth. Start the transformative journey today to ensure a resilient and future-ready workforce.

EXECUTIVEness in the digital age demands digital literacy, adaptability, and a continuous learning mindset. Now is the time for you to lead by example, embracing new digital tools, staying open to innovative technologies, and fostering a culture of continuous learning. This adaptation extends beyond personal growth; it ensures that organizations remain agile in an ever-changing digital landscape.

> GREAT LEADERS EMBRACE TECHNOLOGICAL FORCES WITH A CLEAR UNDERSTANDING OF WHY THEY MATTER, HOW THEY CAN BE APPLIED STRATEGICALLY, AND HOW THEY TIE INTO THE PRINCIPLES OF *EXECUTIVENESS*, SEIZING THE OPPORTUNITIES THESE TRENDS PRESENT WHILE PROACTIVELY ADDRESSING THE CHALLENGES THEY ENTAIL.

12.4 Adapting to the Digital Age: Skillsets and Mindsets for Technologically Savvy Leadership

Even if my words edge toward redundancy, it's important to emphasize that you should equip yourself with a foundational understanding of technology, its capabilities, potential, opportunities, and challenges.

This chapter explores the essential attributes that enable leaders to navigate the digital age successfully and lead their organizations toward sustainable growth and innovation.

Digital Literacy: Empowering Innovative Leadership

Digital literacy is no longer an add-on skill; it's a foundational element of modern leadership. Leaders who harness the power of digital literacy stand poised to revolutionize industries, spark innovation, and drive their organizations to new heights. Here's why digital literacy is the cornerstone of innovative leadership:

When leaders are digitally literate, they can envision novel ways to harness technology to their advantage. They see beyond the surface and tap into the vast potential technology offers. For instance, a digitally literate leader might envision leveraging blockchain technology not just for cryptocurrencies but also to revolutionize supply chain management, ensuring transparency and efficiency.

Digital literacy equips you with the ability to identify and optimize processes. Whether it's streamlining internal workflows or revolutionizing customer experiences, you can adapt technology to enhance processes and think outside the box. You now understand that technology isn't a one-size-fits-all solution but a toolkit for solving diverse challenges. This mindset encourages creative problem-solving and the exploration of unconventional solutions.

Take the case of Uber, which disrupted the traditional taxi industry by leveraging mobile technology to connect riders with drivers seamlessly. This out-of-the-box thinking transformed not only transportation but also the gig economy.

> DIGITAL LITERACY EMPOWERS YOU TO TRANSFORM INDUSTRIES, DRIVE INNOVATION, AND PIONEER NOVEL SOLUTIONS. IT ENABLES YOU TO HARNESS TECHNOLOGY AS A CREATIVE FORCE, ADAPT AND ENHANCE PROCESSES, AND THINK BEYOND THE CONVENTIONAL BOUNDARIES OF THEIR FIELD.

As leaders continue to navigate the digital age, digital literacy isn't just an asset; it's the engine of visionary leadership. In today's rapidly changing digital landscape embracing change is a constant. You can no longer view change as an occasional disruption but as an ever-present force driving innovation.

Agility is a hallmark of digitally savvy leaders. Your capacity to pivot and adapt are strengths in a world where unforeseen circumstances can alter the course of a business overnight.

EXECUTIVEness embodies adaptability, making sure everyone understands that change is an opportunity for growth.

By fostering an environment that celebrates innovation, knowing that the most groundbreaking ideas are born out of change and disruption, you establish yourself Superior Leader. Failure isn't a roadblock but a stepping stone toward progress and resilience plays a significant role in an unpredictable terrain where challenges are inevitable.

IN ESSENCE, DIGITAL LITERACY AND ADAPTABILITY NOT ONLY ALLOWS YOU TO SURVIVE BUT THRIVE IN THIS EVER-EVOLVING LANDSCAPE. FOR YOU, CHANGE IS AN ALLY, NOT AN ADVERSARY, AND YOU LEVERAGE IT TO DRIVE INNOVATION, GROWTH, AND LASTING SUCCESS.

12.5 Leveraging Technology for Effective Leadership: Strategies for Integration and Impact

Superior Leadership today has transcended traditional boundaries. Effective executives harness technology as a powerful ally, enabling them to enhance communication, foster collaboration, and make data-driven decisions with precision.

Here are some ideas on how you could leverage technology for impactful leadership, accompanied by real-world case studies that exemplify these principles.

Enhancing Communication:

Effective communication is the lifeblood of any organization, and technology offers a myriad of tools to facilitate it. You can leverage digital platforms, such as Slack or Microsoft Teams, to create seamless communication channels. You can also harness video conferencing solutions like Zoom or Microsoft Teams to bridge geographical gaps and conduct face-to-face meetings in a virtual environment. Keep in mind that these tools, now deemed commonplace, were not even considered essential in many organizations just a few years ago.

Case Study: Zoom

During the COVID-19 pandemic, Zoom emerged as a lifeline for businesses and educational institutions worldwide. Zoom's founder and CEO, Eric Yuan, envisioned a platform that not only facilitated remote meetings but also enabled seamless collaboration. Under his leadership, Zoom quickly adapted to meet the surging demand for remote communication, demonstrating the transformative power of technology in enhancing communication.

Fostering Collaboration:

Collaboration lies at the heart of innovation, and technology enables leaders to create virtual workspaces that transcend physical boundaries. Collaboration tools such as Slack, SharePoint or Trello, represent a shift in how we foster collaboration.

Not too long ago, the norm for collaboration revolved around one-on-one meetings, face-to-face interactions and the back and forth exchange of information or documents. Today we have tools that redefine how we collaborate. Whether is a design tool, web platform or financial application, they provide opportunities for seamless collaboration allowing individuals to actively contribute within these platforms. How are you leveraging them?

Working together has taken on a new meaning, thanks to these tools that have transformed the landscape of collaboration, making it more interactive, seamless and inclusive.

Case Study: Slack

Slack, the team communication platform, has redefined how teams collaborate and communicate. Stewart Butterfield, co-founder and CEO of Slack Technologies, recognized the need for a centralized digital workspace. Under his leadership, Slack has become a go-to platform for millions of professionals, streamlining collaboration and knowledge sharing across organizations.

Data-Driven Decision-Making:

In the digital age, leaders can't afford to rely solely on intuition. Data-driven decision-making has become a cornerstone of effective leadership. Leaders can harness tools like Tableau or Power BI to gain insights from vast datasets, enabling them to make informed decisions swiftly.

Case Study: Netflix

Reed Hastings, co-founder and co-CEO of Netflix, transformed the entertainment industry through data-driven decision-making. By analyzing user preferences and viewing habits, Netflix can recommend personalized content to its subscribers. This data-driven approach has not only retained existing customers but also attracted new ones, displaying the immense impact of data in decision-making.

These case studies exemplify how technology can be a formidable asset for leaders when employed strategically.

EFFECTIVE EXECUTIVES UNDERSTAND THAT TECHNOLOGY ISN'T JUST A TOOL; IT'S A CATALYST FOR IMPROVING COMMUNICATION, DRIVING INFORMED DECISIONS AND LEAD WITH IMPACT.

12.6 The Ethical Dimensions of Technology: Navigating Challenges and Maintaining Integrity

Navigating the sea of data is like sailing on a vast and turbulent ocean. The digital era allows us to be equipped with advanced tools to cast our nets into this ocean of information, teeming with opportunities. However, within these promising waters, there are also treacherous waves of compliance and ethics that leaders must navigate.

As technology advances, our capacity to collect data expands. We cast a wide net into the digital ocean, capturing a wealth of customer information. This treasure trove includes everything from customer preferences and online behaviors to transaction histories, location data and much, much more. However, with great data comes great responsibility.

As a marketing compliance leader, I also had to navigate these treacherous waters, seeking the delicate balance between utilizing data to enhance customer experiences and safeguarding their privacy.

Ethics and Marketing:

In my past life as VP of Strategic Marketing & Compliance, one of my teams was tasked with ensuring our data collection and utilization practices for marketing remained within the boundaries of the law and ethics. It wasn't about following rules; it was about adopting a culture of responsibility and trust within the organization while nurturing the creativity regarding the utilization of data to enhance the customer experience.

Even within the complex world of compliance, acknowledging the colossal potential of data to enrich customer experiences was paramount. This recognition underscored the necessity for a creative approach in understanding how to leverage data innovatively, aiming to enhance and personalize, hence the need to question, challenge and expand views.

It was like having a compass that guided us toward creating personalized and engaging interactions. Data allowed us to deeply understand our customers, tailoring our approaches to their unique needs and preferences, and technology provided us the tools to do it in a responsible way.

Our customers needed the reassurance that their data would be used in the most respectable and beneficial way. It was a mutual exchange, where trust was the currency.

This example was a reflection of the principles of *EXECUTIVEness.* Clarity in purpose kept me anchored in the ethical importance of data privacy. Influence through impact enabled me to lead our organization in responsible data utilization.

Yet, as we navigate the waters of data compliance and privacy, another challenge looms: the issue of AI biases. As we increasingly turn to artificial intelligence and machine learning to analyze data, we faced the risk of these technologies perpetuating biases present in the data. It is a reminder that technology, while potent, could also inherit the flaws of the past or flaws of own inclinations.

> TECHNOLOGY AND DATA COULD BE BOTH, POWERFUL ALLIES AND POTENTIAL LIABILITIES, IF TINTED WITH OUR BIASES, PREFERENCES OR INCLINATIONS.

By leveraging data responsibly, recognizing and respecting the "truth" in it, we can identify opportunities for better customer experiences while safeguarding the trust of those who journey with us.

12.7 Translating *EXECUTIVEness* into Action

So far, you've gained insights into how technology and data-driven decision-making are transforming leadership. Now, let's turn these insights into practical actions.

Exercise: Digital Mindset Self-Assessment

- Begin by assessing your digital mindset. Are you open to adopting recent technologies and leveraging data to drive decisions?

- Reflect on your past experiences with technology and data. Have you been resistant to change, or have you embraced opportunities for innovation?

- Identify areas where you can develop a more growth-oriented mindset in the digital age. Set specific goals for expanding your digital horizons, such as learning about emerging technologies or data analytics.

Exercise: Data-Driven Decision-Making

- Take a moment to review your recent decision-making processes. Have you been relying on data to inform your choices?

- Select a recent decision and consider how data could have influenced it. What data sources could have provided valuable insights?

- Going forward, commit to incorporating data-driven decision-making into your leadership style. Identify key data points relevant to your role and industry and make a plan to regularly analyze and apply this data to your decisions.

Exercise: Technological Adaptability

- Reflect on your current level of digital literacy and adaptability. Do you feel confident in navigating and using technology?

- Choose one digital tool or platform that you are less familiar with but could benefit your leadership role. It could be a project management software, data analytics tool, or even a social media platform.

- Dedicate time to learn and experiment with this tool. Seek guidance from colleagues or take online courses if needed. Document your progress and how this newfound knowledge can improve your leadership effectiveness.

Exercise: Ethical Data Use

- Consider the ethical dimensions of data use in your organization. Are there areas where data privacy or biases need further attention?

- Engage with your team or colleagues in a discussion about responsible data utilization. Encourage open dialogue about ethical considerations and brainstorm ways to address potential biases.

- Collaborate with your organization's data experts or ethics committees to ensure that data practices align with ethical standards. Take the initiative to implement or support ethical data policies where necessary.

Exercise: Future-Proofing Your Leadership

- Reflect on your readiness for future technological disruptions. How agile and innovative do you feel in the face of rapid change?

- Set aside time to explore emerging technologies and trends relevant to your industry. Stay informed about developments in AI, automation, or other technological advancements.

- Develop a personal innovation plan that outlines how you will stay adaptable and forward-thinking. Identify areas where you can proactively embrace change and lead your team through technological transitions.

By completing these exercises, you'll be better prepared to navigate technological advancements, make data-driven decisions, and uphold ethical standards, becoming a more impactful and resilient leader.

Chapter 13:

Thriving in a VUCA World - Leading with Agility and Resilience though

In the ever-evolving realm of leadership, I've chosen the acronym VUCA as a reminder of the importance of *EXECUTIVEness*. It's a concise representation of the challenges that today's leaders confront daily – Volatility, Uncertainty, Complexity, and Ambiguity.

13.1 The VUCA Landscape: Navigating Volatility, Uncertainty, Complexity, and Ambiguity

Imagine a world where change is not just constant but occurs at breakneck speed. That's the essence of volatility. Where you'll have to navigate a landscape where predictions have a shorter shelf life than ever before. Uncertainty looms large, casting doubt on the outcome of even well-thought-out plans. Leaders can no longer rely on historical data alone to predict what lies ahead.

Complexity adds another layer of intricacy. Challenges rarely present themselves in isolation. They tend to be part of a broader, intricate web of factors that make solutions elusive.

Lastly, ambiguity clouds the path forward. Decisions that once seemed straightforward now come shrouded in haze. The ambiguity of the situation can make choosing a direction similar to navigating in the dark and no amount of AI can replace the insights and ideas that a well-prepared executive will bring to the table.

> THE VUCA WORLD IS NOT A DOOMED SCENARIO FROM A FUTURISTIC MOVIE; IT'S A LANDSCAPE FULL OF OPPORTUNITIES AND DISCOVERIES, WHERE IMAGINATION, CREATIVITY, AND EVEN A TOUCH OF NAIVETÉ WILL BE VALUED AND DESPERATELY NEEDED.

Innovation and uncharted thinking can be the compass, guiding us through the challenges it will present. Here's where *EXECUTIVEness* steps into the spotlight. Its principles offer a sturdy foundation for leaders traversing the VUCA landscape.

A growth mindset is the first tool in your kit. It encourages a perspective that views challenges as opportunities for growth. With a growth mindset you are better equipped to adapt and innovate, even in the face of adversity.

Adaptability is another essential trait. You can swiftly adjust their strategies based on emerging complexities stand a better chance of thriving amidst the turbulence.

And then there's clarity in purpose. In a world clouded by ambiguity, when you are driven by the 'why' behind your actions, you can navigate with greater integrity and make principled decisions.

As we delve deeper into this VUCA world, it's evident that leadership here demands a unique blend of attributes. This journey ahead will unravel these qualities, offering insights on how to develop and apply them effectively amid volatility, uncertainty, complexity, and ambiguity.

13.2 Balancing Experience and Fresh Perspective: Sustaining Leadership Vitality

Leadership in a VUCA world demands a delicate balance between experience and embracing fresh perspectives. As an experienced executive, you're equipped with a wealth of knowledge gained from years in the field. However, sustaining your leadership vitality requires an open mind, a curious spirit, and a commitment to continuous learning.

In the corporate arena, experience is a valuable asset. It's the collection of lessons learned, challenges overcome, and successes celebrated. It provides a solid foundation on which to build, but it can also become a comfort zone—a place where familiar solutions are readily applied to new problems.

Here's where embracing fresh perspectives comes into play. Open-mindedness, curiosity, and a willingness to learn anew inject vitality into your leadership. It's about acknowledging that the world is evolving, and what worked yesterday might not work tomorrow.

To balance experience with fresh perspectives, consider the following:

Cultivate Curiosity:

Experience executives often have a "been there, done that" mentality. While your experience is invaluable, curiosity fuels innovation. Ask questions, seek out current information, and challenge assumptions. Encourage your team to do the same.

Embrace Diverse Perspectives:

Surround yourself with a diverse team. Diverse perspectives bring forth innovative ideas and solutions. It's not just about hearing different voices; it's about valuing and integrating those voices into your decision-making.

Be a Lifelong Learner:

Commit to continuous learning. Whether it's attending workshops, pursuing further education, or simply reading widely, staying informed about industry trends and emerging technologies keeps your mind agile.

Encourage Experimentation:

Create an environment where experimentation is welcomed. Give your team the freedom to evaluate original approaches, even if they might fail. Learning often arises from failures, and it can lead to breakthroughs.

Mentor and Be Mentored:

Mentorship is a two-way street. Share your wealth of experience and ideas but also be open to learning from others. Don't discard fresh insights and innovative thinking, no matter who is offering them. You'll be surprised!

Challenge the Status Quo:

Be prepared to challenge the status quo, even if your past experiences suggest otherwise. Innovation often comes from disrupting conventional thinking.

By actively incorporating these principles into your leadership approach, you'll find yourself not only balancing your valuable experience with fresh perspectives but also invigorating your leadership vitality. It's the combination of the tried-and-true with the new and innovative that will guide you through the VUCA landscape.

13.3 Resilience and Adaptability: Cornerstones of VUCA Leadership

The unprecedented global pandemic of recent years thrust the world into an era of unexpected volatility, uncertainty, complexity, and ambiguity. Organizations, leaders, and individuals faced challenges that transcended previous boundaries. The business landscape transformed overnight, with remote work becoming the norm, supply chains disrupted, and consumer behaviors shifting unpredictably.

During this trying period, we witnessed a stark contrast between two types of responses. Some organizations and leaders not only weathered the storm but emerged stronger and more innovative than ever. Others, unfortunately, found themselves overwhelmed and unable to adapt, leading to adverse outcomes. The question that arises is: What set these two groups apart?

The answer lies in the twin attributes of resilience and adaptability. While the challenges of the pandemic were unprecedented, they were also an illuminating test of an organization's and leader's ability to navigate the VUCA landscape.

Those who excelled exhibited elevated levels of **resilience and adaptability**, allowing them to survive or even thrive in the face of adversity.

The Resilience Imperative:

Resilience is your capacity to bounce back from adversity and setbacks, emerging stronger and wiser. In a VUCA world, challenges are inevitable. They may come in the form of unexpected disruptions, market volatility, or unforeseen global events. Here's why resilience is paramount:

Navigating Uncertainty - Resilient leaders remain composed and focused amid ambiguity. They lead with confidence, providing stability and reassurance to their teams when everything else seems uncertain.

Turning Setbacks into Comebacks - Resilience enables you to turn setbacks into steppingstones for growth. Instead of being defeated by failure, resilient leaders see it as an opportunity for valuable learning and improvement.

Maintaining Well-Being - The VUCA landscape can be taxing. Resilience extends to personal well-being, ensuring you have the stamina to lead effectively. It's about managing stress, prioritizing self-care, and fostering a healthy work-life balance.

Resilience in Action: Consider the example a mid-sized tech firm.

When the pandemic hit, the leadership swiftly assessed the situation and recognized the need to protect their workforce while maintaining business continuity. They implemented remote work policies, ensured employee safety, and provided mental health resources to address the challenges of isolation and uncertainty.

Through consistent communication and empathy, leaders nurtured a resilient workforce that could weather the emotional and professional challenges of the pandemic. This allowed employees to adapt to the remote work environment and continue delivering results. As a result, the company not only survived but thrived during this period, emerging with a more engaged and resolute team.

The Adaptability Advantage:

Adaptability, on the other hand, is your capacity to adjust to new conditions swiftly and effectively. It's about being flexible and open to change. In a VUCA world, where circumstances can shift rapidly, adaptability offers several advantages:

Swift Response: An adaptable leader can pivot quickly in response to changing circumstances. This agility is crucial for seizing emerging opportunities and addressing unexpected challenges.

Innovation and Growth: An adaptable mindset fosters innovation. It encourages experimentation and exploration, leading to creative solutions and sustained growth.

Team Empowerment: Adaptability isn't just an individual trait; it's a leadership style that can permeate your team. When team members see their leader embracing change, they are more likely to do the same.

Adaptability in Action: Another tech firm faced similar challenges when the pandemic struck.

Here, it's leadership took a different approach. Recognizing the shift in consumer behavior, they swiftly pivoted their product offerings to cater to the emerging needs of the remote workforce and homebound consumers. They repurposed their resources and teams to develop novel solutions and services that aligned with the evolving market.

Their adaptability was evident in its ability to quickly refocus its strategic direction and product roadmap. By embracing change and proactively seeking opportunities within the crisis, they not only mitigated losses but also gained a competitive edge. This allowed the company to emerge from the pandemic as an industry leader with innovative products that addressed the changing needs of their customer base.

These examples illustrate how resilience and adaptability played pivotal roles in shaping the outcomes of two organizations during a challenging period. Resilience enabled the first to maintain employee well-being and stability, while adaptability empowered the second to seize new opportunities and innovate in response to shifting market dynamics.

Both attributes are essential for leaders and organizations navigating the VUCA landscape, as they provide the foundation for not only surviving but thriving in times of uncertainty and change.

Strategies for Building Resilience and Adaptability

While some individuals may naturally possess these traits, resilience and adaptability can also be cultivated and strengthened over time. This section will provide strategies for developing and nurturing these attributes within yourself and your teams. You'll discover actionable steps, practical techniques, and real-world examples of leaders who have exemplified resilience and adaptability in the face of VUCA challenges.

By differentiating these two attributes and focusing on their distinct roles in VUCA leadership, you will acquire a comprehensive understanding of how to thrive and deliver extraordinarily.

13.4 Leading Through Uncertainty: Decision-Making in Complex Environments

In the volatile, uncertain, complex, and ambiguous (VUCA) world that defines our current era, decision-making has become a formidable challenge. Why is this important? The world we operate in today is marked by rapid change, unexpected disruptions, and a constant state of flux. Decisions made by leaders can have profound consequences not only for their organizations but also for society at large.

> DECISION-MAKING IN COMPLEX ENVIRONMENTS ISN'T JUST ABOUT OVERCOMING CHALLENGES; IT'S ABOUT SEIZING OPPORTUNITIES HIDDEN WITHIN THE CHAOS. IT'S A SKILL THAT SEPARATES SUPERIOR LEADERS FROM THE REST.

Exploring Decision-Making Challenges:

Leaders in a VUCA world face a unique set of decision-making challenges, including:

- **Ambiguity:** Critical information is often incomplete or unclear, making it challenging to assess situations accurately.

- **Complexity:** Problems are rarely simple; they are multifaceted and interconnected, requiring a holistic understanding.

- **Uncertainty:** Predicting outcomes becomes increasingly difficult, and the reliability of forecasts diminishes.

- **Volatility:** Rapid and unpredictable changes can disrupt even the most well-thought-out plans.

These challenges highlight the need for leaders to adopt versatile decision-making approaches that can thrive in the face of uncertainty.

Strategies for Making Sound Decisions: Data/Experience and Gut Decision Making:

Some believe that Data driven decision making is the reliable and secure path to good decisions. My belief is that you should not rely on data alone, there are other intangibles to take into account.

My experiences showed me, time over time, that intangibles, such as "gut feeling" and "following your heart" are as valuable and important in the decision-making process as experience and facts. One notable example of a leader blending data, experience, and gut decision-making is the story of Steve Jobs at Apple.

Steve Jobs at Apple:

Steve Jobs, the co-founder and former CEO of Apple Inc., was known for his visionary leadership and his ability to make bold decisions that often defied conventional market research and data analysis. Here's an example:

In 2007, Apple introduced the iPhone, a groundbreaking product that revolutionized the smartphone industry. At that time, market data and research indicated that consumers preferred physical keyboards on their phones. All the major competitors in the smartphone market, including BlackBerry and Nokia, were producing phones with physical keyboards. However, Steve Jobs, drawing from his deep experience in design and technology, as well as his intuitive understanding of consumer desires, decided to go against the data and launch the iPhone with a touchscreen keyboard instead of a physical one. This decision was driven by his belief that touchscreens offered a more intuitive and user-friendly experience.

Jobs famously stated, "You can't just ask customers what they want and then try to give that to them. By the time you get it built, they'll want something new."

The iPhone's immense success not only transformed Apple into one of the world's most valuable companies but also changed the entire smartphone industry.

This approach was a testament to his ability to make groundbreaking decisions by blending data-backed insights (consumer preferences), heart (his deep passion of design and technology), and gut instinct (his intuitive sense of what users would love).

Scenario Planning:

Preparing for multiple potential outcomes and developing contingency plans that can be executed swiftly when needed. Here's a real-life story of how scenario planning played a crucial role for a major corporation:

Shell's Use of Scenario Planning

Shell, one of the world's largest oil and gas companies, is renowned for its effective use of scenario planning. They have been employing this strategic tool since the 1970s to anticipate and adapt to a range of potential future situations in the volatile energy market.

In the early 1970s, Shell began using scenario planning as a response to the global energy crisis and increased market volatility. Traditional forecasting methods were not sufficient to address the complexity and uncertainty in the energy sector.

Here's how Shell's scenario planning worked:

Identifying Key Uncertainties: *Shell's scenario planners identified critical uncertainties, such as geopolitical events, technological advancements, and energy policy changes. These uncertainties had the potential to significantly impact the energy market.*

Developing Multiple Scenario*s: Shell created multiple scenarios or stories about the future, each based on different combinations of these critical uncertainties. These scenarios were not predictions but plausible narratives about futures.*

Exploring Implications: *Shell's leadership and decision-makers explored the implications of each scenario on the company's strategy, operations, and investments. They asked questions like, "What if oil prices skyrocket?" or "What if renewable energy becomes more widespread?"*

Adaptive Strategy: *Based on the insights gained from scenario planning, Shell could develop a more adaptive and resilient strategy. Instead of relying on a single forecast, they could adjust their plans and investments based on the unfolding events that aligned with one of their scenarios.*

One of the most famous instances of Shell's scenario planning was in the 80s when they anticipated the collapse of the Soviet Union and the opening up of Russian oil reserves. This foresight allowed them to be well-positioned to invest in and access these reserves when the opportunity arose.

Shell's success in using scenario planning has made it a classic example of how this approach can help organizations prepare for an uncertain future. It's a testament to how considering multiple futures and their implications can lead to more robust decision-making and strategic planning.

Inclusivity:

Involving diverse perspectives and expertise in decision-making processes to uncover blind spots and challenge assumptions. There are well-known companies that have adopted similar approaches to foster inclusivity and diversity in their organizations. One prominent example is Salesforce:

Salesforce's Approach to Inclusivity and Diversity:

Salesforce, a leading cloud-based software company, recognized the need to enhance diversity and inclusivity within its workforce. While they were committed to equality, they understood that fostering a culture of inclusivity required a more comprehensive strategy.

They set specific goals to increase representation of underrepresented groups in its workforce. For example, they aimed to reach 50% representation of women in the company by a certain year. Salesforce also conducted pay equity assessments to ensure that employees, regardless of gender or ethnicity, were paid equally for equal work. They committed to addressing any disparities found.

CEO Marc Benioff and other top leaders publicly committed to advancing equality within the organization. This commitment helped set the tone for the entire company. As part of their plan, they implemented programs to actively recruit from underrepresented groups, including partnerships with diverse organizations and targeted recruiting efforts. They established ERGs to support employees from diverse backgrounds, including groups like

Boldforce (Black employees) and Outforce (LGBTQ+ employees). These ERGs played a crucial role in creating a sense of belonging.

Salesforce's example demonstrates how a company can take proactive steps to foster inclusivity and diversity, with a commitment from top leadership, clear goals, and a focus on both recruitment and internal support structures like ERGs. Their success not only improved their company culture but also had a positive impact on their business performance and reputation.

Adaptive Leadership:

Embracing adaptability and flexibility in response to evolving circumstances, allowing leaders to pivot when necessary. IBM is a real-life example of a company that embraced adaptive leadership:

IBM's Transformation under Ginni Rometty:

IBM, once known primarily for its hardware and traditional IT services, was facing significant challenges due to changes in the technology industry. When Ginni Rometty took over as CEO in 2012, she recognized that the company needed a dramatic transformation to thrive in a rapidly changing landscape.

Rometty led IBM's transition from a hardware-centric company to a solutions and services provider with a focus on cognitive computing and artificial intelligence (AI). This shift involved a massive change in the company's business model. The company made substantial investments in AI and developed the Watson platform, which became a symbol of their commitment to cognitive computing. Watson was applied across various industries, from healthcare to finance.

IBM strategically acquired companies to bolster its capabilities in cloud computing and data analytics, recognizing the growing importance of these areas. Most importantly, Rometty initiated a cultural shift within IBM, emphasizing innovation, agility, and a growth mindset. She encouraged employees to embrace change and experimentation.

IBM's journey shows how adaptive leadership can enable a company to adapt to change and drive transformation, pivot in the face of disruption, stay relevant in an industry that was rapidly evolving and emerge stronger in a changing landscape.

Continuous Learning:

Cultivating a culture of ongoing learning and reflection to enhance decision-making capabilities over time. Google is real-life example of a company that fostered and succeeded with a culture of continuous learning.

Google's "20% Time" Policy:

Google, known for its innovative and forward-thinking culture, implemented a policy called "20% Time" or "Innovation Time Off." This initiative allowed employees to spend up to 20% of their work hours on projects that interested them personally, even if those projects were unrelated to their primary job responsibilities.

The company believed that granting employees the autonomy to pursue their passion projects would lead to innovation.

"20% Time" provided employees with opportunities to learn new skills and expand their knowledge in areas outside their immediate job roles. Employees were encouraged to explore innovative ideas, technologies, and solutions during their dedicated time.

Google also encouraged employees to share their 20% Time projects with their colleagues, promoting knowledge sharing and collaboration across the organization. The "20% Time" policy at Google led to successful innovations, including Gmail, Google News, and AdSense. These projects were born out of employees' passion for creating something new and their dedication to continuous learning and improvement.

The policy not only resulted in tangible products but also contributed to a culture of learning and curiosity within Google. Employees were empowered to take ownership of their learning journeys and explore new domains, enriching their skill sets.

Google's "20% Time" is a prime example of how a company can foster continuous learning among its employees, leading to both innovation and personal development. It demonstrates the positive impact of giving employees the time and freedom to explore their interests and learn new skills.

> THE ABILITY TO MAKE SOUND DECISIONS IN A VUCA WORLD ISN'T JUST A SKILL; IT'S THE CRUCIBLE IN WHICH GREAT COMPANIES ARE FORGED. IT'S ABOUT TRANSCENDING THE CHAOS AND RECOGNIZING THAT AMIDST UNCERTAINTY, THERE ARE OPPORTUNITIES TO BE SEIZED AND CHALLENGES TO BE SURMOUNTED.

13.5 Agile Leadership: Thriving Amid Change

Today, we find ourselves sailing through a stormy sea, a sea known as VUCA – Volatile, Uncertain, Complex, and Ambiguous. It's a sea where the winds change direction without warning, where the waves rise and fall unpredictably. To navigate these turbulent waters, leaders must embody agility.

Imagine a surfer riding the ocean's waves, each one different from the last. Agile leaders are like those surfers. They don't cling rigidly to predetermined courses or fixed plans. Instead, they flow like water, adapting swiftly to the ever-shifting landscape.

What worked yesterday may not work today. Understand this and be open to change. Don't resist it; ride it. You cannot function as prisoner of the past; become a pioneer of the future.

Effective Communication: The Lifeline

Amid chaos, communication becomes a lifeline. Imagine an orchestra conductor guiding a symphony during a tempest. And you should play a similar role, by harmonizing the efforts of your team or organization, by ensuring everyone is in sync and aligned, even when the environment is noisy and turbulent.

Regardless of the environment or situation, VUCA or not, miscommunication can be disastrous. Prioritizing clear, concise, and transparent communication is necessary, listening actively and empathetically, understanding that a shared understanding is essential for success.

Learning, Unlearning, Relearning

Think of agile leaders as perpetual learners. They see change as an opportunity to gain experience, not a threat to stability. Just as a chameleon adapts its colors to its surroundings, agile leaders adapt their knowledge and skills to the situation at hand.

> UNDERSTAND THAT YESTERDAY'S KNOWLEDGE MIGHT NOT APPLY TODAY - EMBRACE THIS REALITY. THE NEED TO UNLEARN OUTDATED PRACTICES, LEARN NEW ONES, AND CONTINUOUSLY SEEK FRESH PERSPECTIVES IS VITAL. KNOWING THAT LEARNING IS NOT A ONE-TIME EVENT BUT A LIFELONG JOURNEY WILL SET YOU APART.

Agility is not a nice-to-have trait; it's a necessity. Agile executives, like expert surfers, navigate uncertainty with grace, use effective communication as their anchor, and view change as an opportunity for growth.

13.6 Innovative Thinking in VUCA: Navigating Complexity with Creativity

In our journey through the VUCA landscape, we encounter complex challenges that demand innovative thinking. Think of it as an expedition into uncharted territory, where traditional maps are of little use.

The Power of Innovative Thinking

Consider the story of Airbnb, a disruptor in the hospitality industry. Traditional thinking would have led to building more hotels, but Airbnb took a different path. They harnessed the power of innovative thinking by turning people's spare rooms and homes into lodging options. They didn't follow the map; they drew their own.

Innovative thinking is about questioning assumptions, challenging the status quo, and seeing opportunities where others see obstacles. It's the mindset that led to the creation of the sharing economy, revolutionizing how we travel and experience accommodations.

Innovative thinking is cultivated through a culture that values experimentation, rewards creative risk-taking, and provides the space for ideas to flourish. It's not just about having the idea but creating an environment where ideas can take root and grow.

Techniques for Fostering Innovation

Let's borrow a page from Pixar's playbook. They hold regular "Braintrust" meetings where creatives from different departments come together to provide feedback on projects. This cross-pollination of ideas leads to the innovative storytelling we see in Pixar's films.

Brainstorming sessions, cross-functional collaborations, and encouraging diverse perspectives to foster innovative thinking are a few ways you can foster innovation. It's about creating opportunities for serendipitous connections and breakthrough ideas.

Conclusion

As we navigate the complexities of the VUCA landscape, innovative thinking and creativity become our guiding stars. Just as Airbnb reimagined hospitality and Google reshaped our digital lives, when you encourage and harness innovative thinking you will find new paths through the wilderness of uncertainty.

The VUCA world challenges all of us to think differently, and in doing so, we uncover opportunities for innovation that can reshape industries and change the course of history.

13.7 Future-Proofing Leadership in a Rapidly Changing Technological Landscape

The ever-accelerating race of advancement demands future-proofing leadership. Is not a choice; it's a necessity. The speed of change pressures leaders to not only keep pace but also stay ahead, not as a precautionary measure but as a dynamic strategy to thrive in the face of rapid technological disruption.

But what is future-proofing? Future-proofing is the proactive process of equipping leaders and organizations with the agility and resilience needed to navigate uncertainties, anticipate changes and capitalize on emerging opportunities. It involves cultivating a forward-thinking mindset, fostering adaptability and embracing strategic innovation to ensure stained success in an ever-evolving landscape.

And to you, future-proofing could be your commitment to continuous learning and adaptability. It could mean staying attuned to emerging trends and technologies, fostering a workplace culture that encourages innovation and cultivating a team capable of navigating uncertainty with resilience.

Think about embracing change not as a disruption but as an opportunity for grown. Prioritize building diverse and versatile teams, encouraging collaboration and harnessing the power of collective intelligence. Don't forget the importance of strategic foresight - anticipate shifts in the landscape, and proactively position yourself to meet the demand of an ever changing future.

Future-proofing is not about survival; it's about leading with foresight and intentionality in a world of constant transformation. Future-proofing is a strategic imperative supported by tangible actions and successes.

13.8 Translating *EXECUTIVEness* into Action

In the dynamic world of leadership with challenges and rapid technological change, possessing knowledge is not enough; it's about translating that knowledge into tangible action. *EXECUTIVEness* is not a passive state but an active pursuit. This section outlines practical exercises and actionable steps that integrate the core principles discussed in Chapter 13. Here are some exercises and practices to instill and reinforce future-proof leadership:

Exercise: Scenario Planning for Tomorrow

- Objective: Enhance foresight by practicing scenario planning.

- How: Formulate a team to identify potential disruptive scenarios within your industry. Encourage discussions about how each scenario would impact your organization. Develop strategies for responding to these scenarios and staying ahead of the curve.

Exercise: The Resilience Challenge

- Objective: Foster resilience within yourself and your team.

- How: Create a challenge that pushes individuals and teams out of their comfort zones. This could involve tackling a complex problem with limited resources or adapting to a rapidly changing environment. Debrief afterward to extract lessons on adaptability and resilience.

Exercise: The Innovation Sprint

- Objective: Cultivate a culture of innovation and creativity.

- How: Set aside a dedicated period, like a week or a month, for an "Innovation Sprint." Encourage team members to brainstorm creative solutions to existing challenges. Celebrate and reward the most innovative concepts.

Exercise: The Learning Exchange

- Objective: Promote continuous learning within your organization.

- How: Establish a "Learning Exchange" program where team members periodically teach each other new skills or knowledge they've acquired. This could range from technical skills to leadership insights. The act of teaching reinforces learning and promotes a culture of continuous improvement.

By implementing these exercises and practices, you not only solidify the principles of *EXECUTIVEness* discussed in this chapter but also ensure they become ingrained in your leadership approach. Remember, leadership isn't static; it's an ongoing journey of growth and adaptation.

Chapter 14:

Navigating the Future: *EXECUTIVEness* for the Present and Beyond

Within the pages of this book, you've encountered leadership concepts that transcend the conventional. These insights are more than theoretical constructs, they are proven mechanisms of success, which resulted from years of experience studying, embodying and teaching how to excel in the Leadership. The culmination of these elements, all combined, forms the secret sauce that I proudly label *EXECUTIVEness.*

As we journeyed through these chapters, I' didn't just share knowledge; I've revealed insights that challenge conventional leadership paradigms.

> *EXECUTIVENESS*, AS YOU'VE COME TO UNDERSTAND, TRANSCENDS THE WELL-TRODDEN PATHS OF LEADERSHIP LITERATURE. IT EMBODIES A HOLISTIC AND FEARLESS APPROACH, DEMANDING COURAGE, EMPATHY, ADAPTABILITY, AND AUTHENTICITY.

EXECUTIVEness, as I've shared, is the bridge that connects the often-separated domains of strategic thinking and emotional intelligence. It's an approach that acknowledges the importance of empathy and authenticity in leadership, shedding light on the profound impact they have on team dynamics and organizational success.

Moreover, our journey has emphasized the importance of adaptability and resilience. In a world characterized by unpredictability, these qualities aren't just advantageous; they are indispensable. The ability to bend without breaking, to pivot with grace in the face of adversity, is an integral part of effective leadership, one I've shown you can be cultivated.

Infusing these leadership principles into daily practice isn't a mere suggestion but a compelling call to action. Leaders are not confined to boardrooms; they are pioneers, explorers, and mentors. They live out these principles, shaping their daily lives, interactions, and decisions.

We've also recognized the need to navigate the technological landscape with a human-centric approach. The balance between embracing technology's potential and maintaining the human touch is a theme I've emphasized. It's not merely a theoretical discussion; it's a roadmap for leaders seeking to chart a course in the digital age.

And as we ventured into the concept of thriving in a VUCA world, the acronym representing Volatility, Uncertainty, Complexity, and Ambiguity, I've provided practical strategies for leaders not just to survive but to flourish in this challenging environment.

Finally, the chapter on Translating *EXECUTIVEness* into Action was not a mere compilation of exercises; it was an invitation for you to embark on a transformative journey. These exercises and real-world examples serve as the bridge between theory and practice, an opportunity to apply *EXECUTIVEness* in your unique context.

The future of leadership isn't solely found in these insights; it lies in how you choose to embody them. *EXECUTIVEness* isn't a destination; it's a path, a mindset, and a way of being that transcends traditional leadership paradigms. It's a call to become the exceptional leader you were meant to be, one who navigates the present and future with a powerful fusion of skills and emotions.

As you close this book and reflect on the insights shared, ask yourself: How will you elevate your ***EXECUTIVEness*** today to shape the future of your leadership legacy?

Acknowledgements

To my husband, for his steady support through thick and thin. To my family, your endless encouragement and belief in me propel me to aim higher.

To my mentors, your insightful guidance has illuminated my path and enriched my understanding of leadership. Your wisdom is priceless.

To my clients, your stories, your unwavering determination and your successes inspire me to keep pushing the boundaries of leadership. Your unique journeys remind me that leadership is an ever-evolving exploration.

And to my friends and all those who graciously "volunteered" to provide candid feedback, thank you!

This book stands as a testament to the strength of these connections and the transformative power of *EXECUTIVEness.*

About the Author

Patricia Rojas is the founder of Pro Move Solutions, a consultancy dedicated to empowering companies and individuals to reach their fullest potential. With over 20 years in executive roles at Hilton Grand Vacations and Holiday Inn Club Vacations, among others, Pat combines strategic insight with a background in Clinical Psychology to drive transformative growth. She is the creator of the Megaleader 360 Method and the 7 Leadership Patterns Assessment, tools designed to deliver customized solutions that align with each client's vision and goals.

For more on Pat's work and how it can help you or your organization achieve its goals, visit www.patrojas.com